Amazing Geography Facts for Smart Kids
© 2023 by Dr. Leo Lexicon

Check out our fun, auto-themed coloring books

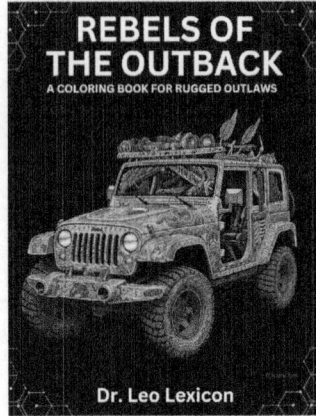

Amazing Geography Facts for Smart Kids

by

Dr. Leo Lexicon

CONTENTS

AMAZING GEOGRAPHY FACTS FOR SMART KIDS

Chapter 1: Asia 2

Chapter 2: Africa 18

Chapter 3: Europe 33

Chapter 4: North America 64

Chapter 5: South America 84

Chapter 6: Australia 104

Chapter 7: Antarctica 130

EXTRA! Free Excerpt from AI for Smart Kids Ages 6-9 148

Amazing Geography Facts for Smart Kids

Welcome to the world of Geography!
Experiencing geographical boredom? Tectonic plates are moving too slow for you, are they? In this awesome book packed with the wackiest geography information imaginable, get ready for the wildest world tour ever!

This book will turn dry geography into an exhilarating rollercoaster ride, and give you some of the most arcane and interesting facts you never knew about the world around us. Whether you consider Africa's "upside-down" baobab tree, or learn about the 5,500 year-old temples of Gozo, you will discover something new on every page.

No textbook could keep it real while containing this much craziness. Let's take geography to the next level!

Dr. Leo Lexicon is an educator and author. He is the founder of Lexicon Labs, a publishing imprint that is focused on creating entertaining books for active minds.

AMAZING GEOGRAPHY FACTS FOR SMART KIDS

Chapter 1: Asia

- Asia is the largest continent, covering about 30% of the Earth's land area.
- Mount Everest, the world's highest peak, is located in Asia.
- The Dead Sea, which is one of the saltiest bodies of water on Earth, is found in Asia.
- The Great Wall of China is visible from space and stretches over 13,000 miles.
- The Caspian Sea, located between Europe and Asia, is the largest enclosed body of water on the planet.
- Asia is home to the world's largest and most diverse rainforest, the Amazon Rainforest.
- Siberia, a region in Russia, is known for its bitterly cold winters, with temperatures dropping as low as -50°C.
- The Gobi Desert, spanning across Mongolia and China, is the coldest desert in the world.
- The longest river in Asia and the third-longest in the world, the Yangtze River, flows through China.

- Japan experiences frequent earthquakes due to its location on the Pacific Ring of Fire.
- The Philippines consists of over 7,000 islands, making it the second-largest archipelago in the world.
- Israel's Dead Sea is so salty that people can easily float on its surface.
- Saudi Arabia's Rub' al Khali, or Empty Quarter, is the largest continuous sand desert on Earth.
- Mongolia is known for its nomadic culture and vast steppes.
- The city of Istanbul, Turkey, straddles two continents: Asia and Europe.
- Sri Lanka is often referred to as the "Teardrop of India" due to its shape on the map.
- The world's tallest building, the Burj Khalifa, is located in Dubai, United Arab Emirates.
- Singapore is one of the world's smallest countries but has one of the busiest ports globally.
- South Korea's capital, Seoul, has the world's fastest internet speeds on average.
- The Maldives is the lowest-lying country in the world, with an average elevation of just 1.5 meters above sea level.
- Kazakhstan is the ninth-largest country globally but has one of the lowest population densities.
- The Bosphorus Strait in Turkey is one of the world's busiest waterways, connecting the Black Sea to the Mediterranean.
- Uzbekistan is home to the ancient city of Samarkand, known for its stunning Islamic architecture.
- Nepal is the birthplace of Siddhartha Gautama, the founder of Buddhism.
- In Turkmenistan, there is a flaming gas crater called the "Door to Hell" that has been burning for decades.
- Bangladesh is one of the most densely populated countries globally, with over 160 million people living in a relatively small area.
- The Maldives is made up of 26 atolls, which are comprised of more than 1,000 coral islands.
- Armenia was the first country to adopt Christianity as its state religion in the early 4th century.
- The world's largest flower, the Rafflesia, can be found in Southeast Asia, particularly Indonesia and Malaysia.

- Mongolia's traditional dwelling is called a "ger" or "yurt," and it is easy to assemble and disassemble, making it ideal for nomadic lifestyles.
- The official name of Thailand is the longest city name in the world: "Krung Thep Mahanakhon Amon Rattanakosin Mahinthara Ayuthaya Mahadilok Phop Noppharat Ratchathani Burirom Udomratchaniwet Mahasathan Amon Piman Awatan Sathit Sakkathattiya Witsanukam Prasit."
- Bhutan measures its success based on a Gross National Happiness index rather than Gross Domestic Product (GDP).
- The Maldives is the flattest country globally, with no point higher than 2.4 meters above sea level.
- Lebanon is one of the world's oldest continuously inhabited countries, dating back over 7,000 years.
- The Philippines is the world's leading producer of coconuts.
- The Aral Sea, once one of the four largest lakes globally, has drastically shrunk due to irrigation projects, becoming a symbol of environmental disaster.
- Iran has one of the world's oldest civilizations, dating back to at least 4000 BCE.
- The ancient city of Petra in Jordan is known as the "Rose City" due to the color of its stone.
- The highest motorable road in the world, Khardung La, is in India's Ladakh region.
- The Great Mosque of Mecca in Saudi Arabia can accommodate up to four million worshipers during the Hajj pilgrimage.
- Indonesia is home to the world's largest lizard, the Komodo dragon.
- The tallest twin towers in the world, the Petronas Towers, are located in Kuala Lumpur, Malaysia.
- The Maldives is the flattest country globally, with no point higher than 2.4 meters above sea level.
- Russia is so large that it spans 11 time zones.
- The world's oldest known civilization, the Sumerians, emerged in what is now Iraq around 4000 BCE.
- The Ural Mountains in Russia are often considered the traditional boundary between Europe and Asia.
- The ancient city of Troy, famous for the Trojan War in Greek mythology, is located in Turkey.
- The United Arab Emirates has the world's tallest hotel, the JW Marriott Marquis Dubai.

- The Indus Valley Civilization, one of the world's earliest urban civilizations, thrived in what is now Pakistan and northwest India around 2600-1900 BCE.
- The world's largest flower, the Rafflesia, can be found in Southeast Asia, particularly Indonesia and Malaysia.
- Mongolia is home to the Bactrian camel, which has two humps, unlike the single-humped dromedary camel found in other parts of the world.
- Japan has over 1,500 earthquakes every year, though most of them are minor and go unnoticed.
- The world's highest battlefield, the Siachen Glacier, is located in the disputed region of Kashmir, between India and Pakistan.
- In the Himalayas, the Yeti is a legendary creature believed by some to inhabit the mountainous regions of Nepal and Tibet.
- The Great Wall of India, also known as the Kumbhalgarh Fort, stretches for 36 kilometers and is the second-longest continuous wall after the Great Wall of China.
- The Philippines has the world's smallest primate, the tarsier, known for its large eyes and unique ability to rotate its head 180 degrees.
- The Taklamakan Desert in China is known as the "Sea of Death" due to its vastness and extreme temperatures.
- Qatar is one of the wealthiest countries globally, with the highest GDP per capita.
- Siberia's Lake Baikal is the deepest and oldest freshwater lake on Earth, containing around 20% of the world's unfrozen surface freshwater.
- The world's largest population of wild camels, the Bactrian camels, can be found in Mongolia's Gobi Desert.
- The Great Wall of China was originally built to protect against invasions by various nomadic groups.
- Bangladesh has the world's largest river delta, formed by the confluence of the Ganges, Brahmaputra, and Meghna rivers.
- The Maldives is the world's lowest-lying country, making it particularly vulnerable to rising sea levels due to climate change.
- Sri Lanka is home to the world's oldest tree, the Sri Maha Bodhi, which is over 2,200 years old.
- Indonesia's Mount Tambora had one of the most powerful volcanic eruptions in recorded history, causing the "Year Without a Summer" in 1816.

- The Korean Peninsula is divided between North Korea and South Korea, with the Demilitarized Zone (DMZ) separating the two countries.
- The Tigris and Euphrates rivers, known as the "cradle of civilization," flow through Iraq and played a crucial role in the development of ancient Mesopotamia.
- The ancient Silk Road was a network of trade routes that connected Asia, Europe, and Africa, facilitating cultural exchange and economic interactions.
- The Dead Sea in Israel and Jordan is so salty that no fish or plants can survive in its waters.
- The unique "Rice Terraces of the Philippine Cordilleras" are a UNESCO World Heritage site, carved into the mountains by indigenous people over 2,000 years ago.
- The Arabian Desert in Saudi Arabia is the largest continuous sand desert in the world.
- South Korea is known for its K-pop music and Korean dramas, which have gained international popularity.
- Iran is home to one of the world's oldest ancient civilizations, the Elamites, dating back to around 2700 BCE.
- The Maldives' economy relies heavily on tourism, and each resort is usually situated on its own private island.
- The ancient city of Babylon, located in present-day Iraq, was once one of the largest and most significant cities in the ancient world.
- Bhutan is the only country globally to measure its success using a Gross National Happiness index.
- The small country of Brunei on the island of Borneo is one of the world's largest exporters of liquefied natural gas (LNG).
- The "Karst Mountains" in China's Guilin region are known for their unique limestone formations and scenic landscapes.
- The island of Jeju in South Korea is famous for its female divers, known as "Haenyeo," who free-dive to harvest seafood without using scuba equipment.
- The Qattara Depression in Egypt is one of the lowest points in Africa and one of the driest places on Earth.
- In Indonesia, there is a sulfuric acid lake called Kawah Ijen, where locals mine sulfur while enduring dangerous conditions.
- Armenia is one of the world's oldest wine-producing regions, with a history of winemaking that dates back over 6,000 years.

- The Dharavi slum in Mumbai, India, is one of the largest slums in Asia, with a population estimated to be over one million people.
- The Land of the Rising Sun, Japan, consists of over 6,800 islands, with Honshu being the largest and most populous.
- The Aral Sea, once the world's fourth-largest lake, has dramatically shrunk due to human activity and is now mostly a salt desert.
- Kazakhstan's Baikonur Cosmodrome is the world's oldest and largest space launch facility.
- The Philippines is the largest producer of coconuts globally, with an average annual production of over 15 million tons.
- Indonesia is home to the world's largest Buddhist temple, Borobudur, which was built in the 9th century.
- The city of Dubai in the United Arab Emirates is known for its ambitious architectural projects, including the artificial Palm Jumeirah island.
- The city of Baghdad, Iraq, was once the center of the Islamic Golden Age and a major hub for scholars, scientists, and philosophers.
- The Maldives' capital, Malé, is one of the most densely populated cities globally.
- The ancient city of Persepolis in Iran was once the ceremonial capital of the Achaemenid Empire.
- The Taklimakan Desert in China is the second-largest shifting sand desert in the world.
- India is home to the world's largest producer of milk, and its buffalo milk is widely used for making dairy products.
- The ancient city of Petra in Jordan was established around 312 BCE and is a UNESCO World Heritage site.
- The Mekong River, one of Asia's longest rivers, flows through several countries, including China, Myanmar, Thailand, Laos, Cambodia, and Vietnam.
- Bhutan is known for its unique system of Gross National Happiness, which prioritizes well-being and sustainable development over economic growth.
- South Korea has one of the world's fastest internet speeds, allowing its citizens to enjoy rapid and reliable internet connections.
- The endangered Bengal tiger is found in the Sundarbans mangrove forest, which spans Bangladesh and India.

- The city of Mecca in Saudi Arabia is the holiest city in Islam and the destination of the Hajj pilgrimage for Muslims worldwide.
- Mongolia's national sport is called "Naadam," which includes competitions in horse racing, wrestling, and archery.
- The Gobi Desert, spanning across Mongolia and China, is home to unique dinosaur fossils, including the discovery of dinosaur eggs in the 1920s.
- India is the world's largest democracy and has more than 2,000 distinct ethnic groups and over 1,600 spoken languages.
- The Indian city of Varanasi is one of the oldest continuously inhabited cities on Earth, dating back over 3,000 years.
- The Al-Ahsa Oasis in Saudi Arabia is the world's largest oasis and a UNESCO World Heritage site.
- The Great Wall of China was initially built over 2,000 years ago but underwent significant expansions and renovations during various dynasties.
- The Philippines has one of the world's most diverse marine ecosystems, with over 2,000 species of fish.
- The Rub' al Khali desert in Saudi Arabia is one of the hottest deserts globally, with temperatures reaching over 50°C.
- South Korea is famous for its love of spicy food, with dishes like kimchi and spicy rice cakes being popular among locals and food enthusiasts worldwide.
- Kazakhstan is the world's ninth-largest country by land area but ranks only 62nd in terms of population density.
- The ancient city of Palmyra in Syria was once an important trading hub along the Silk Road, known for its well-preserved Roman ruins.
- The Mekong River is home to one of the world's largest freshwater fish, the Mekong giant catfish, which can grow up to 10 feet long.
- Bhutan is one of the few countries in the world to ban the use of plastic bags to protect the environment and reduce pollution.
- The Maldives is composed of 26 atolls, which are made up of more than 1,000 coral islands spread across the Indian Ocean.
- Sri Lanka's ancient city of Anuradhapura is home to the oldest human-planted tree on Earth, the Sri Maha Bodhi, which dates back over 2,200 years.
- Indonesia is the world's largest island nation, with over 17,000 islands, and its name "Indonesia" means "Indian Islands."

- The ancient city of Petra in Jordan was featured in the film "Indiana Jones and the Last Crusade."
- Mongolia's "Blue Pearl," Lake Khövsgöl, is one of the largest freshwater lakes in the world and is known for its stunning beauty and crystal-clear waters.
- The Bhutanese government prioritizes environmental conservation and has mandated that at least 60% of the country must remain forested at all times.
- The Caspian Sea is the largest enclosed body of water on Earth, but it is not a sea; it is technically a lake.
- The capital city of South Korea, Seoul, is home to over half of the country's population and is a vibrant and modern metropolis.
- The Philippines has over 36,000 kilometers of coastline, making it the fifth-longest coastline globally.
- Uzbekistan is home to one of the oldest cities in the world, Samarkand, which has a history dating back over 2,700 years.
- The Maldives is the flattest country globally, with an average elevation of only 1.5 meters above sea level.
- Armenia is one of the world's oldest wine-producing regions, and wine has been made there for over 6,000 years.
- The Taklamakan Desert in China is one of the driest places on Earth, and its name means "Place of No Return."
- The Gobi Desert is known for its extreme temperature fluctuations, with hot summers and bitterly cold winters.
- India's Sundarbans is the largest mangrove forest in the world and is home to the elusive and endangered Bengal tiger.
- Turkey's Hagia Sophia, originally built as a cathedral, has served as a church, mosque, and museum throughout its history.
- Japan is made up of 6,852 islands, with the four largest being Honshu, Hokkaido, Kyushu, and Shikoku.
- Bhutan's national sport is archery, and it is an integral part of the country's culture and celebrations.
- The ancient city of Babylon in Iraq was home to one of the Seven Wonders of the Ancient World, the Hanging Gardens of Babylon.
- South Korea's Jeju Island is renowned for its unique volcanic landscape, natural wonders, and distinct culture.
- Israel is home to the lowest point on Earth, the Dead Sea, which is about 430 meters below sea level.
- The Maldives is made up of 26 natural atolls and over 1,000 coral islands, grouped into 20 administrative divisions.

- The ancient city of Petra in Jordan is an architectural marvel, carved into rose-red cliffs by the Nabataeans over 2,000 years ago.
- Uzbekistan's Registan Square in Samarkand is a stunning ensemble of three madrasahs, showcasing intricate Islamic architecture.
- The Philippines has more than 100 ethnic groups and over 170 languages spoken, making it a diverse and culturally rich country.
- The Mekong River is a lifeline for millions of people in Southeast Asia, providing water for irrigation, transportation, and fishing.
- The Armenian alphabet was invented by Mesrop Mashtots in the 5th century and is one of the oldest alphabets still in use.
- Singapore is one of the world's most densely populated countries, with a land area of just 721 square kilometers.
- The Great Wall of China is not a single continuous wall but a series of walls and fortifications built over centuries by various dynasties.
- India is the world's second-largest producer of tea, after China, with Assam being one of its major tea-producing regions.
- The ancient city of Persepolis in Iran was once the ceremonial capital of the Achaemenid Empire and is now a UNESCO World Heritage site.
- The island of Jeju in South Korea is known for its unique volcanic landscape, stunning natural beauty, and abundant marine life.
- Mongolia is known for its rich history and nomadic traditions, with nearly half of the population living a nomadic or semi-nomadic lifestyle.
- The Gobi Desert is home to unique wildlife, including the Bactrian camel, snow leopard, and Gobi bear.
- India's Sundarbans, a UNESCO World Heritage site, is one of the largest mangrove forests in the world and is famous for its Royal Bengal tigers.
- Indonesia's Mount Bromo is one of the most active volcanoes in the world, and visitors can witness spectacular sunrise views from its crater rim.
- The Maldives is composed of 26 atolls, which are made up of over 1,000 coral islands, with less than 200 of them inhabited.
- Sri Lanka is home to the world's oldest wildlife sanctuary, the Yala National Park, which protects diverse flora and fauna, including the Sri Lankan leopard.

- The Philippines is known for its unique transportation called "Jeepneys," originally made from US military jeeps left after World War II and now brightly decorated and used as public transportation.
- South Korea is a leader in technology and is home to some of the world's largest technology companies, including Samsung, LG, and Hyundai.
- Indonesia's Lake Toba, the largest volcanic lake in the world, was formed by a massive eruption that occurred over 70,000 years ago.
- Turkey's Cappadocia region is famous for its otherworldly landscapes, including fairy chimneys and cave dwellings dating back thousands of years.
- India's Ganges River is considered sacred by Hindus and is a pilgrimage destination for millions of devotees each year.
- The ancient city of Palmyra in Syria was once a major trading hub on the Silk Road and was known for its wealth and architectural grandeur.
- Kazakhstan's Baikonur Cosmodrome is the world's first and largest operational space launch facility, from which the first human, Yuri Gagarin, was launched into space.
- The Maldives has an average ground-level elevation of 1.5 meters, making it one of the countries most at risk from rising sea levels due to climate change.
- The unique traditional musical instrument of Mongolia is the Morin Khuur, a horse-head fiddle made from horsehair and wood.
- Singapore is a melting pot of cultures, with a diverse population consisting of Chinese, Malay, Indian, and various other ethnic groups.
- The ancient city of Jericho in Palestine is one of the oldest inhabited cities in the world, dating back over 10,000 years.
- Bhutan is known for its stunning landscapes and is home to several of the world's highest peaks, including Gangkhar Puensum, the highest unclimbed mountain.
- The Maldives' main mode of transportation between islands is by boat, and each island often has its own ferry service.
- The Philippines is home to the world's largest lizard, the Komodo dragon, which can grow up to 10 feet in length.
- Kazakhstan is known for its vast steppes, where nomadic tribes have herded livestock for centuries.

- The Great Wall of China was built to protect against invasions and to regulate trade and immigration along the Silk Road.
- The unique "Sea of Stars" phenomenon occurs in the Maldives, where bioluminescent phytoplankton emit a blue glow in the water at night.
- Uzbekistan's Bukhara is an ancient Silk Road city with well-preserved Islamic architecture, earning it the nickname "City of 1,001 Nights."
- South Korea's Haeinsa Temple houses the Tripitaka Koreana, a collection of Buddhist scriptures carved onto wooden blocks.
- The ancient city of Ephesus in Turkey is home to the Library of Celsus, one of the most impressive libraries of the ancient world.
- The Maldives is one of the world's top destinations for snorkeling and scuba diving due to its stunning coral reefs and abundant marine life.
- The Philippines has over 50 active volcanoes, making it one of the most seismically active countries in the world.
- Indonesia's Mount Rinjani on the island of Lombok is famous for its stunning crater lake called Segara Anak.
- Turkey's Pamukkale is a natural wonder known for its terraces of travertine, formed by mineral-rich hot springs over thousands of years.
- Kazakhstan's Lake Balkhash is one of the largest lakes in the world and is unique because it has a saltwater eastern part and a freshwater western part.
- The Philippines' Tubbataha Reefs Natural Park is a UNESCO World Heritage site and a marine sanctuary with a rich diversity of marine life.
- India's Andaman and Nicobar Islands are known for their pristine beaches, lush rainforests, and diverse indigenous tribes.
- The ancient city of Petra in Jordan is also known as the "Rose City" due to the color of the stone from which it is carved.
- Sri Lanka's Sigiriya Rock Fortress, built in the 5th century, is a UNESCO World Heritage site with impressive ancient frescoes and gardens.
- Bhutan's traditional dress for men is called "Gho," and for women, it is called "Kira," and they are often made of colorful woven fabric.
- The ancient city of Jerash in Jordan is one of the best-preserved Roman ruins outside of Italy.

- Indonesia's Raja Ampat Islands are known for their unparalleled marine biodiversity, with over 1,700 species of fish and 600 species of coral.
- South Korea's Gyeongbokgung Palace is a grand royal palace complex with colorful changing of the guards ceremonies.
- The Philippines is an archipelago of more than 7,600 islands, making it one of the most island-dense countries globally.
- Kazakhstan's Charyn Canyon is often referred to as the "Grand Canyon of Central Asia" and offers stunning landscapes and hiking opportunities.
- India's Taj Mahal is one of the most famous monuments globally and is considered a symbol of eternal love, built by Emperor Shah Jahan in memory of his wife Mumtaz Mahal.
- Uzbekistan's Samarkand is home to the majestic Registan Square, surrounded by three grand madrasahs adorned with intricate tilework.
- The ancient city of Palmyra in Syria was once a vital trading post connecting the Roman and Parthian empires.
- Turkey's Hagia Sophia was originally built as a Christian cathedral, later converted into a mosque, and is now a museum.
- Mongolia's Gobi Desert is one of the world's most significant fossil sites, with the first dinosaur eggs discovered there in the 1920s.
- Singapore's Changi Airport has repeatedly been voted the best airport in the world for its amenities and services.
- The ancient city of Persepolis in Iran was the ceremonial capital of the Achaemenid Empire and is now a UNESCO World Heritage site.
- The Philippines' Bohol Island is known for its unique Chocolate Hills, which turn brown during the dry season, resembling chocolate drops.
- Kazakhstan's Lake Issyk is known for the discovery of an ancient Scythian golden burial mask, now exhibited in the State Hermitage Museum in St. Petersburg, Russia.
- The ancient city of Ephesus in Turkey was once a prominent center of trade and religion in the ancient world, attracting visitors from various civilizations.
- Sri Lanka's Horton Plains National Park is home to "World's End," a stunning cliff with a sheer drop of nearly 1,200 meters.

- The Philippines' Banaue Rice Terraces, often referred to as the "Eighth Wonder of the World," are over 2,000 years old and carved into the mountains by indigenous tribes.
- Uzbekistan's Khiva is an ancient city with well-preserved Islamic architecture, earning it the nickname "Museum City."
- The Maldives is one of the best places on Earth to spot whale sharks, the largest fish in the world.
- Mongolia's Ulaanbaatar, the world's coldest capital city, experiences temperatures as low as -40°C in winter.
- Indonesia's Borobudur Temple is the world's largest Buddhist temple and a UNESCO World Heritage site.
- South Korea is known for its cutting-edge technology and is a leader in the development of 5G networks.
- The Philippines has the world's second-largest archipelago, consisting of more than 7,600 islands.
- India's Sundarbans mangrove forest is the largest mangrove forest globally and is a critical habitat for the endangered Bengal tiger.
- The ancient city of Palmyra in Syria was a vital cultural and economic hub along the Silk Road and was a melting pot of various cultures.
- The Taklamakan Desert in China is known for its shifting sand dunes, which can reach heights of over 500 meters.
- The ancient city of Jericho in Palestine is believed to be one of the oldest continuously inhabited cities in the world.
- Kazakhstan's Baikonur Cosmodrome is the launch site for the Russian Soyuz spacecraft and has been used for space missions since the 1960s.
- The Maldives is one of the world's top luxury travel destinations, known for its overwater villas and pristine beaches.
- India's Konark Sun Temple, shaped like a chariot, is a masterpiece of ancient Indian architecture and a UNESCO World Heritage site.
- Turkey's Grand Bazaar in Istanbul is one of the oldest and largest covered markets in the world, with over 4,000 shops.
- The Philippines is known for its vibrant festivals, such as the Ati-Atihan, Sinulog, and Pahiyas festivals, which showcase colorful parades and cultural performances.
- The ancient city of Palmyra in Syria was once known as the "Bride of the Desert" due to its magnificent architecture and oasis-like setting.

- South Korea's Jeju Island is a UNESCO World Heritage site known for its volcanic landscapes, underground lava tubes, and unique "Stone Grandfather" statues.
- The Maldives is a diver's paradise, with crystal-clear waters, vibrant coral reefs, and abundant marine life, including manta rays and reef sharks.
- Indonesia's Mount Merapi is one of the most active volcanoes in the world and is closely monitored due to its frequent eruptions.
- India's Cherrapunji in the state of Meghalaya holds the record for the highest annual rainfall on Earth.
- The ancient city of Ephesus in Turkey was once a significant center of early Christianity and is home to the ruins of the Temple of Artemis, one of the Seven Wonders of the Ancient World.
- The Philippines has an abundance of unique wildlife, including the tarsier, Philippine eagle, and tamaraw, a critically endangered buffalo species.
- Singapore's Gardens by the Bay is a futuristic park with stunning Supertrees and a massive glass conservatory housing diverse plant species.
- The Maldives is a popular destination for honeymooners, with its romantic overwater villas and secluded beaches.
- Uzbekistan's Bukhara is a UNESCO World Heritage site known for its well-preserved medieval architecture and historic mosques and madrasahs.
- The ancient city of Palmyra in Syria was an important stop on the Silk Road, facilitating trade between the Roman Empire and the East.
- Indonesia's Raja Ampat Islands are often regarded as one of the world's best diving destinations, boasting unrivaled marine biodiversity.
- The Philippines is known for its unique wildlife, such as the tarsier, a small nocturnal primate with enormous eyes.
- Kazakhstan's Lake Balkhash is one of the world's largest lakes and is unique for its brackish water, a mixture of freshwater and saltwater.
- India's Agra Fort, a UNESCO World Heritage site, served as the main residence of the Mughal emperors until the capital moved to Delhi.
- Turkey's Pamukkale terraces are made of white calcium deposits from thermal springs, creating a surreal and picturesque landscape.

- South Korea's DMZ, the Demilitarized Zone, is a heavily fortified buffer zone between North and South Korea, attracting curious visitors from around the world.
- The ancient city of Persepolis in Iran was once the ceremonial capital of the Achaemenid Empire and witnessed grand royal ceremonies and festivals.
- Uzbekistan's Samarkand is home to the Shah-i-Zinda complex, a series of mausoleums with stunning turquoise tilework.
- The Philippines is one of the world's largest exporters of coconuts and coconut-based products.
- Singapore's Changi Airport is known for its innovative and entertaining amenities, including a butterfly garden, movie theaters, and a rooftop pool.
- The Maldives is a favorite destination for snorkeling and diving enthusiasts, with its pristine coral reefs and diverse marine life.
- Indonesia's Mount Bromo is an active volcano known for its otherworldly landscapes and frequently visited for its sunrise views.
- India's Varanasi is one of the oldest continuously inhabited cities in the world and is a sacred pilgrimage site for Hindus.
- The ancient city of Palmyra in Syria was once a prosperous oasis city, thriving on trade and agriculture.
- Turkey's Hagia Sophia, with its impressive dome and stunning mosaics, is a symbol of the city of Istanbul and a testament to Byzantine architecture.
- South Korea's Busan is a vibrant coastal city known for its beautiful beaches, bustling markets, and seafood delicacies.

Chapter 2: Africa

- Africa is the second-largest continent in the world, covering an area of over 30 million square kilometers.
- The Sahara Desert, the largest hot desert globally, spans much of North Africa.
- The Nile River, the longest river in the world, flows through 11 countries in Africa.
- Egypt is home to the Great Pyramid of Giza, one of the Seven Wonders of the Ancient World.
- Africa is the only continent to span all four hemispheres: Northern, Southern, Eastern, and Western.
- Mount Kilimanjaro in Tanzania is the highest freestanding mountain in the world and the tallest mountain in Africa.
- The African continent is home to over 1.2 billion people, representing over 16% of the world's population.

- Madagascar, located off the eastern coast of Africa, is the world's fourth-largest island and is known for its unique biodiversity.
- Africa is the most linguistically diverse continent, with over 2,000 different languages spoken.
- The Serengeti National Park in Tanzania is famous for the annual wildebeest migration, considered one of the most remarkable wildlife spectacles on Earth.
- The Democratic Republic of the Congo is the second-largest country in Africa by land area and is home to the Congo River, the world's second-largest river by discharge volume.
- Africa is believed to be the birthplace of Homo sapiens, with evidence of early human ancestors found in Ethiopia's Omo Valley and South Africa's Cradle of Humankind.
- Nigeria is the most populous country in Africa, with over 200 million people.
- The Kalahari Desert, covering parts of Botswana, Namibia, and South Africa, is known for its red sands and unique wildlife.
- The Maasai Mara National Reserve in Kenya is famous for its high concentration of lions and its role in the annual wildebeest migration.
- Africa is the only continent that crosses the equator, the Tropic of Cancer, and the Tropic of Capricorn.
- Morocco's Atlas Mountains are home to the highest peak in North Africa, Mount Toubkal.
- The African continent is known for its rich mineral resources, including gold, diamonds, copper, and oil.
- The Victoria Falls, located on the border of Zambia and Zimbabwe, is one of the largest waterfalls in the world.
- The African elephant is the largest land animal on Earth, with the savanna elephant being the largest of the three elephant species.
- Africa has the largest concentration of mega-fauna, including elephants, rhinoceroses, lions, and giraffes.
- The Sahara Desert is expanding, with desertification threatening to engulf fertile lands in the Sahel region.
- Ethiopia is one of the oldest countries in the world, with a history dating back over 3,000 years.
- Lake Victoria, shared by Tanzania, Kenya, and Uganda, is the largest tropical lake in the world.

- The Namib Desert in Namibia is home to some of the world's tallest sand dunes, with some reaching heights of over 300 meters.
- The African baobab tree is known for its distinctive swollen trunk and can live for thousands of years.
- Africa is the hottest continent, with temperatures often exceeding 50°C in some regions.
- The Algerian Sahara is home to one of the world's largest underground aquifers, known as the "Great Man-Made River."
- South Africa is home to the iconic Table Mountain, overlooking the city of Cape Town.
- The African lion, often referred to as the "King of the Jungle," is one of the most recognizable symbols of the continent.
- The Sahara Desert was once a lush and fertile region, as evidenced by ancient cave paintings found in Libya's Tadrart Acacus.
- Ethiopia is one of the few countries in Africa to have never been colonized by a European power.
- Lake Tanganyika, bordered by Tanzania, the Democratic Republic of the Congo, Burundi, and Zambia, is the second-deepest lake in the world.
- The African penguin, also known as the black-footed penguin, is found along the southwestern coast of Africa.
- The Nile crocodile, found in various African countries, is one of the largest crocodile species in the world.
- The Sahara Desert is larger than the contiguous United States.
- The baobab tree, found in various African countries, is also known as the "Tree of Life" due to its ability to store water and provide sustenance during droughts.
- The annual migration of over one million wildebeests, zebras, and antelopes between the Serengeti National Park in Tanzania and the Maasai Mara Reserve in Kenya is known as the Great Migration.
- Africa is home to the largest land mammal, the African elephant, and the fastest land mammal, the cheetah.
- The Sahara Desert, known for its extreme temperatures, can reach up to 50°C during the day and drop below freezing at night.
- Lake Malawi, located between Malawi, Tanzania, and Mozambique, is home to more fish species than any other lake in the world.

- Africa is home to some of the world's most iconic animals, including lions, elephants, giraffes, gorillas, and rhinoceroses.
- The Namib Desert in Namibia is considered the oldest desert on Earth, with parts of it estimated to be around 55 million years old.
- The River Nile is not only the longest river globally but also the only major river that flows northward.
- Ethiopia's Danakil Depression is one of the hottest places on Earth, with temperatures often exceeding 50°C.
- The Okavango Delta in Botswana is the largest inland delta in the world, creating a diverse and unique ecosystem.
- The rock-hewn churches of Lalibela in Ethiopia are a UNESCO World Heritage site and a testament to ancient architectural marvels.
- Africa is the most linguistically diverse continent, with thousands of distinct languages spoken among its diverse cultures.
- The African grey parrot is one of the most intelligent bird species, known for its ability to mimic human speech.
- Madagascar is home to several unique species, including lemurs, chameleons, and the world's smallest chameleon.
- The Atlas Mountains in North Africa extend across Morocco, Algeria, and Tunisia and are one of the region's major mountain ranges.
- Africa's Lake Baikal in Russia is the deepest freshwater lake in the world, reaching depths of over 1,600 meters.
- The Masai Mara National Reserve in Kenya is named after the Maasai people, who have a rich cultural heritage.
- Africa has an extensive coastline, spanning over 30,000 kilometers and providing access to the Atlantic, Indian, and Southern Oceans.
- The African elephant is known for its excellent memory and complex social structure, making it one of the most intelligent animals on the planet.
- Africa is home to numerous ancient civilizations, including Egypt, Nubia, Kush, Carthage, and the Kingdom of Aksum.
- The Serengeti National Park in Tanzania is a UNESCO World Heritage site and hosts the largest terrestrial mammal migration in the world.

- Africa's Mount Nyiragongo in the Democratic Republic of the Congo is one of the most active volcanoes, known for its lava lake.
- The African continent is the most genetically diverse region globally, with significant genetic variation among its population.
- The traditional art of African tribes includes intricate beadwork, wood carvings, masks, and vibrant textiles.
- Africa's Kalahari Desert is home to the San people, known for their unique clicking language and ancient hunter-gatherer lifestyle.
- The Nile crocodile, found in various African countries, is one of the largest crocodile species in the world.
- Africa has a rich history of ancient trade routes, such as the Trans-Saharan trade route, which facilitated the exchange of goods and cultures across the continent.
- The Maasai people of East Africa are known for their distinctive red clothing and unique customs, including traditional jumping dances.
- Africa is home to a vast array of wildlife, including the Big Five: lions, elephants, buffalos, leopards, and rhinoceroses.
- The Democratic Republic of the Congo is home to the second-largest rainforest in the world, after the Amazon rainforest.
- Africa has some of the world's most stunning natural wonders, such as Victoria Falls, the Sahara Desert, and the Ngorongoro Crater.
- The Swahili language, widely spoken in East Africa, is a Bantu-based language with significant Arabic influence.
- Africa has a rich tradition of storytelling through oral traditions, passing down history, culture, and moral lessons through generations.
- The Namib Desert in Namibia is famous for its massive sand dunes, some of which can reach heights of over 300 meters.
- Africa's baobab trees are known for their massive trunks and unique shape, often referred to as "upside-down trees."
- The Maasai Mara National Reserve in Kenya is home to an abundance of wildlife, including the famous wildebeest migration.
- The Sahara Desert is not entirely made up of sand dunes; it also includes rocky plateaus, gravel plains, and salt flats.

- The red dunes of Sossusvlei in Namibia are some of the tallest sand dunes in the world and create a mesmerizing landscape.
- Africa's Nile crocodile is one of the few species of crocodiles that can survive in both freshwater and saltwater environments.
- The Okavango Delta in Botswana is a unique inland delta, fed by the Okavango River, and supports a wide variety of wildlife.
- Africa's Sahara Desert is one of the hottest places on Earth, with temperatures exceeding 50°C in some areas.
- The San people of the Kalahari Desert are among the oldest surviving hunter-gatherer tribes in the world, with a rich cultural heritage.
- Africa has some of the world's most famous archaeological sites, such as the ancient city of Carthage in Tunisia and the pyramids of Giza in Egypt.
- The Ethiopian Highlands are known for their stunning landscapes, including rugged mountains, deep valleys, and fertile plateaus.
- Africa's Lake Victoria is the largest lake on the continent and the second-largest freshwater lake in the world.
- The Nile River is considered the primary water source for many countries in North and East Africa.
- Africa's Lake Tanganyika is the second-deepest lake globally, after Lake Baikal in Russia.
- Lake Tanganyika is estimated to be around 10 million years old and is a vital habitat for numerous unique fish species.
- The Sahara Desert is so vast that it covers an area of about 9.2 million square kilometers, making it nearly as large as the entire United States.
- Africa's Congo River has the second-largest discharge of any river in the world, surpassed only by the Amazon River.
- The Congo River Basin is home to the world's second-largest tropical rainforest, after the Amazon rainforest.
- Africa has a diverse range of ecosystems, including savannas, rainforests, deserts, mountains, and grasslands.
- The African continent is home to more than 2,000 species of birds, making it a birdwatcher's paradise.
- Africa has an abundance of natural resources, including gold, diamonds, oil, and natural gas.
- The African elephant is not only the largest land animal but also one of the most intelligent, with the ability to display complex emotions and use tools.

- Africa's Serengeti ecosystem is one of the oldest and most complex ecosystems in the world, supporting an incredible diversity of plant and animal life.
- Africa has over 85% of the world's elephants, making it a critical region for elephant conservation efforts.
- The Great Rift Valley, stretching from Mozambique to the Red Sea, is the largest geological feature on the African continent.
- The African continent is home to some of the world's most iconic mammals, including the lion, giraffe, cheetah, and hippopotamus.
- Africa's Atlas Mountains, running across Morocco, Algeria, and Tunisia, were formed by the collision of the African and Eurasian tectonic plates.
- Africa has the largest population of cheetahs in the world, but the species is classified as vulnerable due to habitat loss and human-wildlife conflict.
- The African lion is considered the king of the animal kingdom and is a symbol of strength and pride.
- Africa's Cape Verde archipelago is unique as it is the only country in the world that is named after the Cape Verde Peninsula on the West African coast.
- Africa's Madagascar is known for its high level of endemism, with the majority of its plant and animal species found nowhere else on Earth.
- Africa's Kalahari Desert is not a true desert but rather a semi-arid savanna, characterized by its red sands and vast grasslands.
- Africa has some of the world's most significant salt pans, including the Makgadikgadi Pans in Botswana and the Danakil Depression in Ethiopia.
- The African buffalo is one of the "Big Five" game animals and is known for its fierce and unpredictable nature.
- The African grey parrot is one of the most popular and sought-after pet birds due to its intelligence and ability to mimic speech.
- The Congo River is the second-longest river in Africa, after the Nile, and it flows through a vast and ecologically rich region.
- Africa's Mount Kilimanjaro, the highest mountain on the continent, is a dormant volcano and one of the most iconic landmarks in Africa.
- Mount Kilimanjaro is famous for its three volcanic cones: Kibo, Mawenzi, and Shira.

- Africa's Great Zimbabwe is an ancient stone city that was once the capital of the Kingdom of Zimbabwe, an important trading center in the 11th to 15th centuries.
- The African leopard is known for its ability to climb trees, making it an agile and elusive predator.
- Africa's Lake Victoria is the world's largest tropical lake and is shared by three countries: Kenya, Uganda, and Tanzania.
- The African savanna is a vast grassland ecosystem teeming with wildlife, including large herds of wildebeests, zebras, and antelopes.
- The Okavango Delta in Botswana is the largest inland delta in the world and provides a haven for a diverse range of wildlife.
- Africa is the second-most populous continent, with over 1.3 billion people, and is projected to have the largest population growth in the coming decades.
- The African civet is a small, nocturnal mammal known for producing the musk used in perfumes.
- Africa's Mount Elgon, located on the border between Kenya and Uganda, is an ancient extinct volcano with the largest surface area of any volcanic crater in the world.
- The African penguin, also known as the jackass penguin, makes distinctive donkey-like braying sounds, leading to its nickname.
- The Congo Basin rainforest is the second-largest tropical rainforest on Earth, providing habitat for numerous rare and endangered species.
- Africa's Baobab Avenue in Madagascar is a famous avenue lined with massive baobab trees, creating a surreal and iconic landscape.
- The African leopard is known for its exceptional climbing ability and often carries its prey into trees to avoid scavengers.
- The African wild dog, also known as the painted wolf, is one of the most successful predators, with a unique social structure and cooperative hunting techniques.
- Africa's Lake Malawi is home to an incredible array of cichlid fish species, making it a popular destination for freshwater aquarium enthusiasts.
- Africa's Sahara Desert is not entirely covered in sand; it also contains vast rocky plateaus and gravel plains.
- The African elephant plays a crucial role in shaping its environment through activities such as digging water holes and clearing pathways.

- Africa's Congo Basin rainforest is second only to the Amazon rainforest in terms of its biodiversity and ecological importance.
- Africa's Drakensberg Mountains in South Africa are renowned for their dramatic peaks, deep valleys, and unique rock formations.
- The African wild dog has one of the highest hunting success rates among large carnivores, with success rates exceeding 70%.
- Africa's Mount Kenya is the second-highest mountain on the continent and is a UNESCO World Heritage site.
- Africa is home to some of the world's most famous archaeological sites, such as the ancient city of Carthage in Tunisia and the rock-hewn churches of Lalibela in Ethiopia.
- Africa's Congo Basin is home to the critically endangered western lowland gorilla, one of the two subspecies of gorillas.
- The African elephant's trunk is a highly versatile tool, capable of delicate tasks like picking up small objects and powerful enough to uproot trees.
- Africa's Mount Ruinsori, located on the border between Uganda and the Democratic Republic of the Congo, is famous for its equatorial snow.
- The African buffalo is considered one of the most dangerous animals in Africa and is known for its aggressive behavior.
- Africa's Congo Basin rainforest is known as the "second lungs of the Earth" due to its crucial role in absorbing carbon dioxide and producing oxygen.
- The African elephant's large ears serve to regulate body temperature by radiating excess heat.
- The Sahara Desert is not only the hottest but also one of the driest deserts in the world, with some regions receiving no rain for years.
- Africa's Namib Desert is home to the famous "Fairy Circles," mysterious circular patches devoid of vegetation.
- The African baobab tree's fruits are known as "monkey bread" and are edible, containing high levels of vitamin C.
- The Congo River's immense flow releases an estimated 1.2 million cubic meters of water per second, equal to about 10% of the world's total river flow.
- Africa's Mount Kilimanjaro has multiple climate zones, from tropical rainforest at the base to arctic conditions at the summit.
- The African elephant's tusks are elongated incisor teeth made of ivory, which has sadly made them targets of illegal poaching.

- The Sahara Desert's sand dunes can reach heights of over 180 meters, equivalent to the height of a 60-story building.
- Africa's Nile crocodile is an opportunistic predator and is known for its ambush hunting technique.
- The Congo Basin rainforest is home to over 400 species of mammals and 10,000 species of plants.
- Africa's Namib Desert is home to the Welwitschia mirabilis, a peculiar plant known for its long, strap-like leaves and extreme longevity.
- The African lion is the only big cat species that forms social groups, known as prides.
- Africa's Mount Kenya has three main peaks, with Batian being the highest at 5,199 meters above sea level.
- The African wild dog's scientific name, Lycaon pictus, translates to "painted wolf," referring to its unique coat pattern.
- The Sahara Desert's sandstorms, known as "haboobs," can reach heights of up to 1,000 meters and can cover vast areas.
- Africa's Congo Basin rainforest is estimated to be around 150 million years old, making it one of the oldest forests in the world.
- The African leopard's spots, called rosettes, help it blend into its surroundings and remain camouflaged.
- Africa's Lake Victoria is the largest tropical lake in the world by surface area, covering approximately 68,800 square kilometers.
- The Congo River Basin is one of the most significant reservoirs of freshwater biodiversity on Earth.
- The African baobab tree can live for thousands of years, and some individuals have been known to reach an age of over 6,000 years.
- The Sahara Desert's temperature can vary dramatically, with daytime temperatures exceeding 50°C and nighttime temperatures dropping below freezing.
- Africa's Okavango Delta is a UNESCO World Heritage site and an essential wetland habitat for numerous bird species.
- The African elephant's complex social structure includes matriarchal family groups and strong bonds among herd members.
- Africa's Congo River has a total length of approximately 4,700 kilometers, making it the second-longest river in Africa.
- The African buffalo has never been domesticated and is considered one of the "Big Five" game animals in Africa.

- Africa's Namib Desert is famous for its "dancing dunes," which appear to move and change shape due to the wind.
- The African leopard is a solitary and elusive predator, relying on stealth and surprise to catch its prey.
- Africa's Lake Malawi contains more fish species than any other lake globally, making it a biodiversity hotspot.
- The Congo River Basin is home to the critically endangered eastern lowland gorilla, one of the two subspecies of gorillas.
- The African wild dog has unique color patterns, with a mixture of black, yellow, and white patches on its coat.
- Africa's Victoria Falls, located on the border of Zambia and Zimbabwe, is one of the Seven Natural Wonders of the World.
- The Sahara Desert's sand dunes can change shape and position due to the wind, constantly reshaping the landscape.
- Africa's Congo Basin rainforest is home to several endangered species, such as the bonobo and the okapi.
- The African baobab tree's fruit is not only edible but also has medicinal properties, being used to treat various ailments.
- Africa's Nile crocodile is an apex predator, known to prey on a wide variety of animals, including fish, birds, and mammals.
- The African elephant's skin is highly sensitive and can be several centimeters thick in certain areas.
- Africa's Mount Kilimanjaro is a stratovolcano, and its summit is covered in snow and ice, making it a challenging climb.
- The Sahara Desert's sand dunes can be as large as small mountains, with some reaching heights of over 500 meters.
- The Congo River is a lifeline for many communities, providing water, food, and transportation.
- The African leopard is a nocturnal hunter, using its keen senses and excellent vision to hunt at night.
- Africa's Namib Desert is home to a wide variety of desert-adapted animals, including oryx, springbok, and desert elephants.
- The African wild dog has specialized vocalizations, including distinctive sounds called "hoo" and "chirr," which they use to communicate within their pack.
- Africa's Lake Malawi, also known as Lake Nyasa, is one of the world's most biodiverse freshwater lakes, hosting over 1,000 species of colorful cichlid fish.
- The Sahara Desert's sand dunes can move at a rate of up to 50 feet per year, creating shifting landscapes.

- Africa's Congo Basin rainforest is so dense that sunlight barely reaches the forest floor, creating a unique and intricate ecosystem.
- Africa's Victoria Falls is one of the world's most significant waterfalls, with a width of 1,708 meters and a height of 108 meters.
- The Sahara Desert's sand dunes can create distinct patterns, such as barchans (crescent-shaped dunes) and seif dunes (longitudinal dunes).
- Africa's Okavango Delta is home to the African fish eagle, an iconic bird known for its majestic call and impressive fishing skills.
- The African leopard's spots are unique to each individual, allowing researchers and conservationists to identify and track them.
- The Sahara Desert's sand dunes can create a phenomenon known as the "Saharan dust," where fine particles are carried by the wind across continents, affecting weather patterns and air quality.
- Africa's Congo River has numerous islands, including the largest river island in the world, Ilha do Bananal, located in Brazil but part of the Amazon basin.
- The African elephant's trunk contains over 100,000 muscles, allowing for precise movements and incredible strength.
- The African buffalo is known for its unique behavior of "mobbing" predators, where a group of buffalo will collectively defend themselves against predators like lions.
- Africa's Okavango Delta supports a diverse range of wildlife, including large herds of elephants, buffalo, and antelope.
- The African wild dog is one of the most social carnivores, living in tight-knit packs led by an alpha pair.
- Africa's Victoria Falls is locally known as "Mosi-oa-Tunya," which translates to "the smoke that thunders," due to the massive spray and roar created by the falling water.
- Africa's Congo Basin rainforest plays a vital role in regulating the Earth's climate by sequestering carbon dioxide and releasing oxygen through photosynthesis.
- The Congo River Basin contains a vast network of tributaries and streams, creating one of the world's most extensive river systems.

- Africa's Okavango Delta is a vital habitat for various bird species, including the iconic African fish eagle and the elusive Pel's fishing owl.
- The Sahara Desert's sand dunes can reach heights of over 500 feet, creating an awe-inspiring landscape.
- Africa's Lake Malawi is nicknamed the "Calendar Lake" due to its approximate length of 365 miles and a width of 52 miles.
- The Congo River is the second-longest river in Africa and the deepest river globally, with depths reaching up to 220 meters.
- The African elephant's large ears serve to dissipate heat, helping them regulate their body temperature in hot climates.
- Africa's Okavango Delta is an oasis in the desert, attracting an incredible variety of wildlife during the dry season.
- The African buffalo has a reputation for being unpredictable and dangerous, especially when wounded or threatened
- Africa's Lake Tanganyika is home to a unique fish called the Tanganyika sardine, which can be found at depths of over 700 meters.
- The African baobab tree's trunk can store massive amounts of water, making it a crucial resource for both humans and animals during droughts.
- Africa's Nile crocodile has a unique gland in its mouth that allows it to excrete excess salt, enabling it to survive in both freshwater and saltwater environments.
- The Okavango Delta is often referred to as the "jewel of the Kalahari" due to its lush beauty and abundant wildlife.
- Africa's Serengeti National Park is home to the critically endangered black rhinoceros, one of the most threatened species in the world.
- The African elephant's tusks continue to grow throughout their lifetime, with the longest tusks reaching up to 3 meters in length.
- Africa's Lake Malawi contains more fish species than any other lake globally, making it a paradise for divers and fish enthusiasts.
- The African wild dog has a unique hunting strategy, where members of the pack take turns chasing and wearing down their prey until it becomes exhausted.
- Africa's Victoria Falls creates a massive plume of mist that can be seen from miles away, earning it the nickname "the smoke that thunders."

- The Sahara Desert's sand dunes can reach speeds of up to 40 kilometers per hour during sandstorms, covering large areas in a short time.
- Africa's Okavango Delta is a paradise for birdwatchers, hosting over 400 bird species, including rare and colorful birds like the African jacana and malachite kingfisher.
- The African leopard is a skilled climber, often dragging its prey into trees to avoid scavengers and other predators.
- Africa's Lake Malawi is renowned for its stunning diversity of cichlid fish, with more than 1,000 species found in its waters.

Chapter 3: Europe

- Europe is the second-smallest continent in terms of land area, spanning about 10.18 million square kilometers.
- The continent is home to over 740 million people, making it the third-most populous continent.
- Europe is known for its diverse languages, with over 200 languages spoken across the continent.
- Vatican City, located in Rome, Italy, is the smallest independent state in the world and serves as the spiritual center of the Roman Catholic Church.
- Europe is famous for its rich history and is often referred to as the "cradle of Western civilization."
- The continent is home to some of the world's oldest universities, including the University of Bologna in Italy, founded in 1088.
- Europe is home to the world's largest beer festival, Oktoberfest, held annually in Munich, Germany.

- The European Union (EU) is a political and economic union of 27 European countries, aimed at promoting peace, stability, and cooperation.
- Europe's longest river is the Volga, flowing through Russia and spanning approximately 3,690 kilometers.
- The continent is known for its breathtaking castles, with some of the most famous examples found in Germany, France, and the Czech Republic.
- Europe is home to the world's largest inland body of water, the Caspian Sea, located between Europe and Asia.
- Finland is often referred to as the "land of a thousand lakes," but in reality, it has around 188,000 lakes within its borders.
- The Tower of Pisa in Italy is famously known for its leaning structure, caused by a poorly laid foundation.
- Europe is home to some of the world's most scenic train rides, such as the Glacier Express in Switzerland and the Flam Railway in Norway.
- The continent is known for its ancient and mystical landmarks, including Stonehenge in England and the Acropolis in Greece.
- Europe has a rich tradition of fairy tales, with famous authors like Hans Christian Andersen and the Brothers Grimm originating from the continent.
- The European Union's flag has 12 golden stars on a blue background, representing unity and solidarity among its member states.
- Iceland, known as the "Land of Fire and Ice," has both glaciers and active volcanoes within its unique landscape.
- Europe is home to the world's smallest country, Monaco, which is less than two square kilometers in size.
- The continent is known for its mouthwatering cuisine, including pasta and pizza from Italy, croissants from France, and bratwurst from Germany.
- Europe's largest national park is Vatnajökull National Park in Iceland, covering over 12,000 square kilometers.
- The Eiffel Tower in Paris, France, was initially constructed as a temporary exhibit for the 1889 World's Fair but became a permanent landmark due to its popularity.
- Europe has a diverse range of landscapes, from the snowy peaks of the Alps to the stunning fjords of Norway.

- The European Space Agency (ESA) is a leading organization in space exploration and research, working collaboratively with other countries worldwide.
- The continent has a rich cultural heritage, with 37 UNESCO World Heritage Sites in Italy alone.
- The Northern Lights, also known as the Aurora Borealis, can be observed in several European countries, including Norway, Sweden, and Finland.
- Europe is known for its vibrant art scene, with famous museums like the Louvre in Paris and the British Museum in London.
- The continent is home to some of the world's most prestigious fashion capitals, including Paris, Milan, and London.
- Europe's highest peak is Mount Elbrus in Russia, standing at approximately 5,642 meters above sea level.
- The continent is known for its historic and picturesque villages, such as Hallstatt in Austria and Giethoorn in the Netherlands.
- The Euro is the official currency used by 19 of the 27 European Union member countries.
- Europe is famous for its many music festivals, including Glastonbury in the UK and Tomorrowland in Belgium.
- The continent is home to the longest railway tunnel in the world, the Gotthard Base Tunnel in Switzerland, spanning over 57 kilometers.
- The Nobel Prizes, awarded for outstanding achievements in various fields, were established by the will of Alfred Nobel, a Swedish inventor and scientist.
- Europe's diverse geography includes both arctic regions in Scandinavia and Mediterranean climates in Southern Europe.
- The continent has a rich literary history, with famous authors like William Shakespeare from England and Leo Tolstoy from Russia.
- Europe's Mediterranean region is known for its delicious cuisine, including Greek moussaka, Italian pasta, and Spanish paella.
- The continent has a wealth of historical landmarks, including the Colosseum in Rome, the Parthenon in Athens, and the Tower Bridge in London.
- Europe's largest inland delta is the Danube Delta, located in Romania, and is a haven for birdwatchers and nature enthusiasts.

- The continent has a long history of monarchy, with several royal families still in existence, such as the British Royal Family and the Spanish Royal Family.
- The first modern Olympic Games were held in Athens, Greece, in 1896, reviving the ancient tradition of athletic competitions.
- Europe is home to some of the world's most famous composers, including Ludwig van Beethoven, Wolfgang Amadeus Mozart, and Johann Sebastian Bach.
- The continent is known for its vibrant Christmas markets, with some of the most popular ones located in Germany and Austria.
- Europe's largest island is Greenland, an autonomous territory of Denmark, and it is the world's largest island in terms of land area.
- The continent is home to several UNESCO Geoparks, such as the Azores Geopark in Portugal and the Harz-Braunschweiger Land-Osterode Geopark in Germany.
- Europe's smallest country by population is Vatican City, with only around 800 residents.
- The University of Oxford in the UK and the University of Cambridge in the UK attract students from all over the world.
- Europe has a wide range of languages, with over 60 indigenous languages spoken in the Caucasus region alone.
- The Black Forest in Germany is famous for its dense woodland and picturesque scenery, inspiring fairy tales and legends.
- Europe's most prominent river is the Volga, flowing through Russia and spanning approximately 3,690 kilometers.
- The Principality of Sealand, located off the coast of England, is a micronation housed on an abandoned World War II sea fort.
- The island of Sark in the Channel Islands is one of the last places in the world where cars are banned, and transportation is primarily by bicycle or horse-drawn carriage.
- The city of Venice, Italy, is built on a series of over 100 small islands and is famous for its intricate network of canals.
- The Kingdom of Denmark is the oldest monarchy in Europe, with a history dating back over a thousand years.
- The country of Liechtenstein is one of the world's smallest countries, and its capital, Vaduz, has a population of approximately 5,500 people.
- The Åland Islands, an autonomous region of Finland, are home to the last remaining fleet of windjammers, tall ships used for commercial trade in the 19th and early 20th centuries.

- The island of Gozo, part of Malta, is home to one of the world's oldest free-standing temples, the Ggantija Temples, dating back over 5,500 years.
- The Principality of Monaco is the world's most densely populated country, with over 19,000 people per square kilometer.
- The country of Andorra, situated between France and Spain, has one of the longest life expectancies in the world, with an average life span of over 80 years.
- The world's northernmost capital city is Reykjavik, Iceland, known for its geothermal activity and stunning landscapes.
- The tiny town of Santa Claus Village, located in Rovaniemi, Finland, is known as the official hometown of Santa Claus.
- The Isle of Man, a self-governing British Crown Dependency, has its own unique language called Manx Gaelic, which is closely related to Irish and Scottish Gaelic.
- The Vatican Secret Archives, located in Vatican City, is one of the most extensive and secretive historical archives in the world, housing documents dating back over 1,000 years.
- The Karkonosze Mountains, also known as the Giant Mountains, straddle the border between Poland and the Czech Republic and are home to the mythical figure of Rübezahl, a trickster spirit of the mountains.
- The village of Bourtange in the Netherlands was once a fortified military settlement and has been restored to its 18th-century appearance, drawing visitors to experience life in the past.
- The independent city-state of San Marino claims to be the world's oldest surviving republic, with a history dating back to 301 AD.
- The ruins of the ancient city of Pompeii, buried by the eruption of Mount Vesuvius in 79 AD, provide a fascinating glimpse into Roman life and architecture.
- The Hall of Mirrors at the Palace of Versailles in France contains 357 mirrors and is famous for being the location of the signing of the Treaty of Versailles, which ended World War I.
- The capital of Cyprus, Nicosia, is the last divided capital city in the world, with the "Green Line" separating the Greek and Turkish Cypriot areas.
- The Kingdom of Spain is home to the oldest restaurant in the world, "Restaurante Botín," which has been operating since 1725.

- The country of Switzerland is known for its diverse landscapes, with four official languages: German, French, Italian, and Romansh.
- The Romanian Palace of the Parliament, also known as the People's House, is the world's heaviest building, weighing approximately 4.1 million tons.
- The island of Svalbard, located in the Arctic Ocean, is home to the Global Seed Vault, a secure repository storing seeds from around the world in case of a global catastrophe.
- The Kingdom of Sweden has a "Freedom to Roam" law, allowing anyone to explore and camp on private land as long as they do not disturb the landowner.
- The Republic of Ireland is known for its ancient Celtic heritage, with many traditional practices and festivals still celebrated today.
- The unique limestone formations of the Burren in Ireland create a surreal landscape, often described as a "lunar" or "alien" landscape.
- The country of Montenegro is home to Europe's deepest canyon, the Tara River Canyon, reaching a depth of over 1,300 meters.
- The city of Mostar in Bosnia and Herzegovina is famous for its iconic Stari Most (Old Bridge), a UNESCO World Heritage Site and a symbol of reconciliation after the Bosnian War.
- The Principality of Liechtenstein has a postal museum that operates its own philatelic bureau, producing a wide variety of colorful and unique stamps.
- The island of Sicily, an autonomous region of Italy, is home to Mount Etna, one of the world's most active volcanoes.
- The Republic of San Marino is one of the world's oldest constitutional republics and claims to have the world's oldest constitution, adopted in 1600.
- The Hermitage Museum in St. Petersburg, Russia, is one of the largest and oldest museums in the world, housing over three million works of art.
- The country of Cyprus is home to the world's oldest wine still in production, Commandaria wine, dating back over 5,000 years.
- The city of Riga, the capital of Latvia, is famous for its extensive collection of Art Nouveau architecture, making it one of the best-preserved Art Nouveau cities in the world.

- The unique rock formations of the Meteora in Greece are home to six active monasteries, perched atop towering sandstone pillars.
- The country of Estonia has one of the highest rates of internet usage in the world, and in 2005, it became the first country to allow online voting in parliamentary elections.
- The Aeolian Islands, located off the coast of Sicily, are named after Aeolus, the Greek god of winds, due to the strong winds often experienced in the region.
- The city of Brussels, Belgium, is famous for its delicious chocolate and has more chocolatiers per square kilometer than any other city in the world.
- The medieval village of Český Krumlov in the Czech Republic is a UNESCO World Heritage Site, known for its well-preserved architecture and picturesque river views.
- The Republic of Slovenia is home to the world's oldest wooden wheel, dating back over 5,000 years, found in a marsh near Ljubljana.
- The island of Gotland in Sweden is known for its unique medieval wall paintings, preserved in the churches of Visby and showcasing scenes from daily life during the Middle Ages.
- The country of Luxembourg is one of the world's smallest countries, and it is the only Grand Duchy remaining today.
- The Valaam Monastery in Russia is located on Valaam Island in Lake Ladoga and is famous for its peaceful and picturesque setting.
- The country of Georgia is home to the world's oldest-known winery, dating back over 8,000 years.
- The city of Lviv in Ukraine has a vibrant café culture, with over 2,500 coffeehouses, making it one of the coffee capitals of Europe.
- The Aran Islands in Ireland are known for their unique knitting tradition, with the famous Aran sweaters featuring intricate patterns that represent different families and clans.
- The city of Brasov in Romania is home to the narrowest street in Europe, Strada Sforii, which measures only 1.32 meters wide.
- The Belgian city of Ghent has an unusual tradition where residents gather in public squares to throw bread rolls at each other during the "Throwing of the Bread Rolls" festival.

- The country of Malta has a prehistoric underground burial site known as the Hypogeum of Hal-Saflieni, believed to be the world's oldest underground temple.
- The city of Glasgow in Scotland has more green spaces per capita than any other city in the UK.
- The country of Finland is known for its quirky competitions, such as the Wife Carrying World Championships and the Mobile Phone Throwing World Championships.
- The village of Plougastel-Daoulas in France holds an annual strawberry-themed treasure hunt, where participants decode clues hidden in murals to find a treasure chest of strawberries.
- The country of Bosnia and Herzegovina is home to the Stari Most Bridge in Mostar, known for hosting an annual diving competition where daredevils jump from the bridge into the icy waters of the Neretva River.
- The Greek island of Lesbos is the birthplace of the famous poet Sappho, known for her romantic and lyrical poetry.
- The Kingdom of Norway is home to the world's longest road tunnel, the Lærdal Tunnel, which spans over 24.5 kilometers.
- The Estonian island of Kihnu is known for its unique matriarchal society, where women hold many traditional roles, including being captains and sailors.
- The city of Tallinn in Estonia has the world's first public Christmas tree display, dating back to 1441.
- The Romanian region of Transylvania is famous for its medieval castles and folklore, including the legend of Count Dracula.
- The country of Moldova has the world's largest wine cellar, Mileștii Mici, with over 2 million bottles of wine.
- The city of Trieste in Italy has its own unique cuisine, influenced by its diverse cultural heritage and historical connections with Austria and Slovenia.
- The Latvian town of Sabile is home to the world's northernmost vineyard, where locally produced wines are made from cold-resistant grape varieties.
- The Italian island of Sardinia has one of the highest concentrations of centenarians in the world, known for its residents' longevity.
- The city of Edinburgh in Scotland is home to the Camera Obscura, one of the oldest surviving visitor attractions in the world, offering panoramic views of the city.

- The country of Cyprus is known for its ancient copper mines, dating back over 4,000 years, which played a crucial role in trade and commerce during antiquity.
- The Spanish town of Buñol hosts the annual "La Tomatina" festival, where participants engage in a massive tomato fight, using over 150,000 kilograms of tomatoes.
- The Faroe Islands, an autonomous territory of Denmark, have more sheep than people, with approximately 70,000 sheep and a population of around 50,000.
- The city of Porto in Portugal is famous for its production of Port wine, a fortified wine that is aged in cellars along the Douro River.
- The country of Latvia is home to the Great Ķemeri Bog, a vast marshland with wooden boardwalks that offer visitors a chance to explore its unique flora and fauna.
- The Greek island of Naxos is home to the ancient "Portara," a massive marble gate that remains as the entrance to an unfinished temple dedicated to the god Apollo.
- The village of Gimmelwald in Switzerland is car-free, and visitors can only access it by cable car or hiking.
- The country of Georgia is known for its unique alphabet, which has 33 letters and is one of the oldest continuously used scripts in the world.
- The small village of Midsomer Norton in England inspired the fictional setting for the popular British TV series "Midsomer Murders."
- The Norwegian town of Hell has a railway station, making it possible for visitors to take a train to Hell and back.
- The country of Liechtenstein has a strong postal service and issues unique postage stamps, some of which are even made of wood or embroidered fabric.
- The British territory of Gibraltar is home to the only wild monkey population in Europe, the Barbary macaques.
- The Swedish town of Köping has an annual "Bläckfisken" (Squid) festival, where the local community gathers to celebrate and enjoy seafood.
- The Italian island of Sicily has the world's oldest known puppet theater, known as "Opera dei Pupi," dating back to the 19th century.

- The city of Dublin in Ireland is home to the Chester Beatty Library, housing an extensive collection of rare manuscripts, prints, and artifacts from around the world.
- The German island of Heligoland is known for its unique red cliffs and is one of the few places in Germany where seals can be observed in their natural habitat.
- The country of Andorra is famous for its medieval architecture, with many well-preserved villages and castles.
- The island of Malta is home to the world's oldest known human-built structures, the megalithic temples, dating back over 5,000 years.
- The Belgian town of Binche hosts the traditional "Gilles of Binche" carnival, where participants wear elaborate costumes and wooden clogs and throw oranges to the crowd.
- The city of Copenhagen in Denmark has an extensive network of cycling paths, and bicycles outnumber cars in the city.
- The Czech Republic is known for its ancient astronomical clock in Prague, the "Prague Orloj," which dates back to the 15th century.
- The island of Spitsbergen, part of the Svalbard archipelago, is one of the few places in the world where it is illegal to die, due to the permafrost preventing decomposition.
- The Irish town of Athlone has an annual "World Custard Pie Throwing Championship," where participants compete in throwing pies at each other.
- The country of Slovenia is home to the unique "Lipizzaner" horses, known for their performances at the Spanish Riding School in Vienna, Austria.
- The Romanian town of Sibiu is known for its stunning architecture and was designated the European Capital of Culture in 2007.
- The Greek island of Crete is believed to be the birthplace of the ancient Minoan civilization, one of the oldest in Europe.
- The city of Berlin in Germany has a unique green space known as "Teufelsberg," a man-made hill constructed from the rubble of World War II.
- The city of St. Petersburg in Russia is home to the quirky "Bottle House," a unique building constructed entirely from over 50,000 glass bottles.
- The Scottish island of Eigg is powered entirely by renewable energy, making it one of the world's greenest islands.

- The country of Belgium is home to the "Atomium," a unique building shaped like an iron crystal and originally constructed for the 1958 Brussels World's Fair.
- The Romanian village of Buzescu is known for its extravagant houses, featuring vibrant colors, elaborate designs, and intricate decorations.
- The Croatian town of Hvar is famous for its fields of lavender, used to produce fragrant lavender products like oils and sachets.
- The city of Istanbul, Turkey, straddles two continents, with the Bosphorus Strait dividing the European and Asian sides.
- The town of Sintra in Portugal is known for its fairytale-like palaces and castles, including the colorful Pena Palace.
- The country of Luxembourg is one of the founding members of the European Space Agency (ESA) and has its own space mining law.
- The island of Gotland in Sweden hosts an annual "Medieval Week" festival, where participants dress in historical costumes and reenact medieval life.
- The city of Bruges in Belgium has a unique tradition of brewing "Brugse Zot," a beer with its own branded glassware shaped like a clown's hat.
- The country of Iceland has a unique belief in elves, trolls, and other mystical creatures, and many roads and buildings are intentionally designed to avoid disturbing their supposed habitats.
- The Greek island of Patmos is known as the "Island of the Apocalypse" because it is believed to be the place where Saint John received the visions described in the Book of Revelation.
- The Danish island of Møn is home to the "Dark Sky Park," offering stunning views of the night sky and a chance to witness the Northern Lights.
- The country of Monaco is known for its lavish Grand Prix, a Formula 1 race that takes place on the city streets of Monte Carlo.
- The Scottish town of Dunkeld hosts an annual "Haggis Hurling World Championship," where participants compete in throwing haggis, a traditional Scottish dish made from sheep's offal.
- The Republic of San Marino has its own unique international calling code, "+378," and is one of the few countries in the world to have its own telephone country code.

- The Czech Republic is home to the "Bone Church" in Kutná Hora, a chapel decorated with human bones and skulls.
- The city of Plovdiv in Bulgaria is one of the oldest continuously inhabited cities in Europe, with a history dating back over 6,000 years.
- The British territory of Gibraltar is home to the only airport runway in the world intersecting an active road, the Winston Churchill Avenue.
- The city of Naples in Italy is known for its unique pizza culture, with traditional Neapolitan pizza designated as a UNESCO cultural heritage.
- The country of Finland is home to the "Moomin Museum," dedicated to the beloved Moomin characters created by Finnish author Tove Jansson.
- The Hungarian town of Hódmezővásárhely has a quirky tradition of hosting "Busójárás," a carnival where people wear elaborate masks and costumes to scare away winter.
- The British territory of Gibraltar is home to the Barbary macaques, the only wild monkeys in Europe.
- The town of Shetland in Scotland hosts an annual "Up Helly Aa" festival, where participants dress as Vikings and carry a replica longship through the streets before setting it ablaze.
- The French town of Annecy is known as the "Venice of the Alps," with its network of canals and picturesque bridges.
- The island of Lanzarote in the Canary Islands is home to the unique "Jameos del Agua," a series of natural caves transformed into an underground concert hall and bar.
- The country of Malta has a tradition of colorful fishing boats known as "luzzus," adorned with symbols and eyes for protection against evil spirits.
- The town of Zalipie in Poland is famous for its unique folk art tradition of painting colorful floral patterns on houses, fences, and even dog houses.
- The Swedish island of Öland is home to the Borgholm Castle, which hosts a unique annual opera festival inside its ruins.
- The British territory of Gibraltar has its own unique species of wildflowers, including the Gibraltar candytuft and the Gibraltar campion.
- The city of Split in Croatia is built around the ancient Diocletian's Palace, a UNESCO World Heritage Site that serves as a living part of the city's historic center.

- The country of Andorra has a tradition of "Bordas," traditional stone buildings used by shepherds as shelter during the grazing season.
- The village of Colmar in France is known for its colorful half-timbered houses and is often considered one of the most beautiful towns in Europe.
- The island of Gran Canaria in the Canary Islands is home to the "Maspalomas Dunes," a unique desert-like landscape next to pristine beaches.
- The British territory of Gibraltar is home to a unique species of wild monkeys called Barbary macaques, the only wild monkeys in Europe.
- The city of Lviv in Ukraine has an underground network of tunnels and catacombs that were used for various purposes throughout history, including as escape routes and storage spaces.
- The Danish town of Skagen is famous for its unique natural phenomenon called the "Skagen Odde," where the North Sea and the Baltic Sea meet, creating a visible line between the two bodies of water.
- The country of Cyprus is home to the "Cyprus donkey," a small and sturdy breed of donkey that has been used for centuries in agriculture and transportation.
- The island of Gotland in Sweden has its own unique dialect, Gotlandic, which differs significantly from the Swedish spoken on the mainland.
- The Romanian town of Bistrița is believed to be the inspiration for the fictional town of Bistritz in Bram Stoker's novel "Dracula."
- The city of Thessaloniki in Greece is home to the unique "Umbrellas" installation, where colorful umbrellas are suspended above the streets, creating a vibrant and whimsical atmosphere.
- The country of San Marino has its own unique motorsport event called the "Races of the Republic," where drivers compete in a challenging hill climb race.
- The Scottish town of Dull has an official "twinning" with the American town of Boring, creating the humorous partnership of "Dull and Boring."
- The city of Nîmes in France is home to the "Maison Carrée," one of the best-preserved Roman temples in the world.

- The Estonian island of Kihnu has its own unique women's culture, recognized as a UNESCO Intangible Cultural Heritage, where women have historically held significant social and cultural roles.
- The town of Tropea in Italy is famous for its red onions, known for their unique sweetness and used in local cuisine.
- The country of San Marino has a unique military tradition of annually changing the "Captain Regents," who jointly serve as the heads of state.
- The Finnish town of Rovaniemi is known as the "Official Hometown of Santa Claus," and it attracts visitors from around the world to experience the magic of Christmas.
- The city of Inverness in Scotland is believed to be the home of the Loch Ness Monster, known as "Nessie," one of the world's most famous cryptids.
- The Italian town of Alberobello is known for its unique "trulli" houses, traditional dry-stone huts with conical roofs, designated as a UNESCO World Heritage Site.
- The Faroe Islands, an autonomous territory of Denmark, are home to a unique form of domesticated sheep known as "Faroe sheep," famous for their gentle temperament.
- The Republic of Ireland is known for its fascinating folklore, including mythical creatures such as leprechauns, banshees, and selkies.
- The Greek island of Ikaria is one of the world's five "Blue Zones," areas where people are known for their longevity and healthy lifestyles.
- The city of Salzburg in Austria is famous for its connection to the musical "The Sound of Music," and visitors can take tours to visit the filming locations.
- The British territory of Gibraltar is home to the "Gibraltar Candytuft," a unique flowering plant found only in the region.
- The Norwegian town of Nusfjord is an exceptionally well-preserved fishing village and a UNESCO World Heritage Site.
- The city of Bath in England is famous for its Roman-built baths, which have been used for over 2,000 years for their supposed healing properties.
- The country of Montenegro is home to the unique "Lady of the Rocks," a man-made island and church created by sinking old ships and filling them with rocks.

- The Spanish town of Cadaqués is known for its picturesque white houses and was a favorite spot for artists like Salvador Dalí and Pablo Picasso.
- The British territory of Gibraltar is home to unique wildlife, including the Barbary macaques, dolphins, and several species of migrating birds.
- The Estonian town of Viljandi hosts an annual "Folk Music Festival," where participants celebrate traditional Estonian music and culture.
- The city of Rotterdam in the Netherlands has a unique tradition of celebrating "Koninginnedag" (Queen's Day), now known as "Koningsdag" (King's Day), with massive outdoor parties and flea markets.
- The country of Cyprus is known for its unique wine-making technique called "Commandaria," producing a dessert wine with a history dating back over 5,000 years.
- The Greek island of Crete has its own unique dialect, Cretan Greek, which is distinct from standard Greek and includes many ancient words and expressions.
- The city of Edinburgh in Scotland is home to the "Stone of Destiny," a symbol of Scottish royalty and coronation ceremonies.
- The country of San Marino has one of the highest rates of centenarians per capita in the world, with a significant number of residents living past 100 years of age.
- The Italian island of Stromboli is known for its active volcano of the same name, which has been erupting continuously for over 2,000 years.
- The city of Girona in Spain has a unique tradition called "El Caganer," where nativity scenes include a figure of a man defecating, representing fertility and good luck.
- The Danish town of Billund is the birthplace of the LEGO toy company, and visitors can explore the original LEGOLAND theme park.
- The French town of Rocamadour is built into a steep cliffside and is famous for its religious significance and pilgrimage route.
- The city of Dublin in Ireland has a unique tradition of serving "coddle," a dish made from bacon, sausages, and potatoes, often enjoyed after a night out.

- The Romanian region of Maramureş is known for its unique wooden churches, designated as a UNESCO World Heritage Site.
- The Swedish town of Mora hosts an annual "Vasaloppet," the world's oldest and longest cross-country ski race, covering 90 kilometers.
- The Italian town of Santa Maria di Leuca is the southernmost point of the Apulia region, and it is where the Adriatic and Ionian Seas meet.
- The city of Bath in England is famous for its Georgian architecture, and the entire city is designated as a UNESCO World Heritage Site.
- The Estonian island of Saaremaa is known for its unique "Kaali crater," one of the rarest forms of impact craters created by a meteorite impact.
- The British territory of Gibraltar has a unique form of government known as the "Westminster-style democracy," based on the British political system.
- The Portuguese town of Evora is home to the unique "Capela dos Ossos" (Chapel of Bones), where the walls and ceiling are adorned with human bones.
- The Scottish town of Kirkwall is home to the St. Magnus Cathedral, known for its remarkable medieval architecture.
- The country of Cyprus is famous for its unique breed of cat known as the "Cyprus cat," which has a distinctive tail resembling a pom-pom.
- The city of Delft in the Netherlands is famous for its iconic blue and white pottery, known as "Delftware."
- The Scottish town of Pitlochry hosts an annual "Enchanted Forest," a light and sound event set in a mystical forest.
- The island of Madeira, an autonomous region of Portugal, is famous for its unique "levada" irrigation system, featuring a network of channels that distribute water across the landscape.
- The city of Cluj-Napoca in Romania is known as the "Treasure City," due to its long history of holding significant collections of art and artifacts.
- The British territory of Gibraltar is home to the "Gibraltar Barbary macaque," the only wild monkey population in Europe.
- The town of Røros in Norway is known for its well-preserved wooden architecture and its historical copper mines.

- The Estonian town of Paide hosts an annual "Paide Battle of the War Choirs," where different choirs battle each other by singing songs to impress the judges.
- The country of Malta is known for its unique cart ruts, ancient tracks carved into the limestone bedrock that have puzzled archaeologists for centuries.
- The British territory of Gibraltar has a unique postal code system, with addresses using the letters GX11.
- The German town of Goslar is home to the "Kaiserpfalz Goslar," an imperial palace that was once the residence of Holy Roman Emperor Henry III.
- The Italian town of Cefalù is known for its unique "lumie," candlelit boats that light up the sea during religious processions.
- The country of Slovakia has a unique tradition of "Kraslice," elaborately decorated Easter eggs made using a wax-resist technique.
- The island of Sylt in Germany is known for its unique culinary tradition of "Salzwiesenlamm," lamb raised on the salt marshes.
- The Spanish town of Sitges hosts an annual "Carnaval," known for its outrageous costumes and vibrant celebrations.
- The city of Cardiff in Wales is home to the "Animal Wall," a decorative wall at Cardiff Castle featuring sculptures of various animals.
- The Swedish island of Öland is famous for its "Ölandsblomman," a flower-shaped symbol used to represent the island.
- The Republic of Ireland is known for its unique traditional music, including the distinctive sounds of the uilleann pipes and the bodhrán drum.
- The Italian island of Elba is famous for being the site of Napoleon Bonaparte's first exile after his abdication.
- The Norwegian town of Flåm is home to the "Flåm Railway," one of the steepest standard-gauge railways in the world.
- The city of Belfast in Northern Ireland has a unique political mural tradition, with large-scale murals reflecting the region's history and culture.
- The Greek island of Kos is believed to be the birthplace of the ancient physician Hippocrates, considered the father of medicine.
- The French town of Amiens is home to the "Cathédrale Notre-Dame d'Amiens," one of the largest Gothic cathedrals in France.

- The city of Bristol in England is famous for its street art scene, with works by renowned street artist Banksy adorning its walls.
- The island of Alderney, part of the Channel Islands, is known for its unique breed of cow, the "Alderney cow."
- The city of Basel in Switzerland is home to the "Tinguely Fountain," a kinetic sculpture fountain created by artist Jean Tinguely.
- The Portuguese town of Monsanto is known for its houses built among and under giant boulders.
- The Swedish island of Gotland hosts an annual medieval festival known as "Medeltidsveckan," where participants dress in historical costumes and celebrate medieval culture.
- The city of York in England has a unique tradition called "The Shambles," a historic street with overhanging timber-framed buildings.
- The Austrian town of Hallstatt is famous for its picturesque Alpine setting and is often considered one of the most beautiful villages in Europe.
- The country of Latvia is home to a unique celebration called "Jāņi," where people gather to welcome the summer solstice with bonfires, singing, and dancing.
- The Italian town of Deruta is known for its unique ceramics and maiolica pottery, with intricate designs and vibrant colors.
- The British territory of Gibraltar has its own unique breed of monkey known as the "Barbary macaque," the only wild monkey population in Europe.
- The German town of Würzburg is home to the "Würzburger Stein," a historic vineyard producing some of the world's finest wines.
- The city of Granada in Spain is famous for the stunning Alhambra palace, a UNESCO World Heritage Site.
- The Estonian town of Tartu is home to the "Kissing Students" fountain, where locals believe that kissing near the fountain brings good luck in exams.
- The Croatian town of Hvar is known for its lavender fields, producing high-quality lavender products like oils and perfumes.
- The country of Slovenia is home to a unique species of cave-dwelling "olm" salamander, also known as "human fish" due to its pale skin.

- The Greek island of Delos is a UNESCO World Heritage Site and is believed to be the birthplace of the gods Apollo and Artemis.
- The city of Varna in Bulgaria is home to the "Varna Necropolis," one of the oldest known burial sites in the world.
- The Italian island of Stromboli is famous for its "Strombolian eruptions," frequent and relatively mild volcanic eruptions.
- The British territory of Gibraltar is home to unique rock formations, known as the "Pillars of Hercules," which have mythological significance.
- The Danish town of Ribe is the oldest existing town in Denmark, with a history dating back over 1,300 years.
- The Croatian town of Hum is officially recognized as the world's smallest town, with a population of around 30 people.
- The island of Sardinia, Italy, is known for its unique nuraghe structures, ancient stone towers built by the Nuragic civilization.
- The Spanish town of Oviedo is known for its unique tradition of "carbayones," sweet pastry treats shaped like oak leaves.
- The island of Guernsey, part of the Channel Islands, has its own unique breed of cow, the "Guernsey cow."
- The city of Ljubljana in Slovenia has a unique tradition of "Zmajček" (Little Dragon), a legendary creature that represents the city's spirit and identity.
- The Romanian town of Alba Iulia is home to the "Alba Carolina Citadel," one of the largest citadels in Romania.
- The country of Luxembourg has a unique national dish called "Judd mat Gaardebounen," consisting of smoked pork collar with broad beans.
- The island of Sark in the Channel Islands is one of the few places in the world where cars are banned, and transportation is mainly by horse-drawn carriages and bicycles.
- The city of Vilnius in Lithuania is known for its unique artistic tradition of "Angel's Wings," street art installations that feature large angel wings.
- The Greek island of Mykonos is famous for its iconic windmills, which have become symbols of the island.
- The Italian town of Otranto is home to a unique "Tomb of the Martyrs," where the bones of 800 martyrs are displayed in an intricate mosaic pattern.

- The Faroe Islands, an autonomous territory of Denmark, have a unique tradition of celebrating "Ólavsøka," a national holiday featuring boat races, concerts, and traditional sports.
- The Spanish town of Bilbao is home to the "Guggenheim Museum Bilbao," an iconic modern art museum designed by architect Frank Gehry.
- The island of Sylt in Germany has its own unique dialect, Söl'ring, which is distinct from the mainland German language.
- The British territory of Gibraltar is home to unique flora and fauna, including several species of orchids and migratory birds.
- The Estonian town of Rakvere hosts an annual "Tarzan Race," where participants compete in an obstacle course inspired by the legendary character Tarzan.
- The city of Riga in Latvia is home to the "Cat House," a building with two cat sculptures on its roof, which were placed there to mock a rival merchant.
- The island of Santorini in Greece is famous for its stunning sunsets, attracting visitors from around the world.
- The French town of Lourdes is known for its religious significance and is one of the most popular pilgrimage destinations in the world.
- The Scottish town of Dunvegan is home to Dunvegan Castle, the oldest continuously inhabited castle in Scotland, dating back over 800 years.
- The city of Aarhus in Denmark has a unique tradition of celebrating "Aarhus Festuge," a week-long cultural festival with music, arts, and performances.
- The Romanian town of Sighișoara is known for its well-preserved medieval citadel and is a UNESCO World Heritage Site.
- The British territory of Gibraltar is known for its unique honey production, with locally produced honey made from a variety of wildflowers.
- The city of Rovaniemi in Finland is officially recognized as the "Official Hometown of Santa Claus," and visitors can meet Santa and his reindeer year-round.
- The Czech town of Český Krumlov is home to a unique "Baroque Theater," one of the few remaining original Baroque theaters in the world.
- The Italian town of Barga is known for its strong Scottish ties and holds an annual "Barga Scottish Festival."

- The Greek island of Corfu is home to the "Kumquat," a small citrus fruit that has become a symbol of the island.
- The German town of Quedlinburg is famous for its well-preserved medieval architecture and is a UNESCO World Heritage Site.
- The country of San Marino has its own unique football team, which is not a member of FIFA but has its own football association.
- The Danish island of Fanø is famous for its unique tradition of "Fanø Kniplingsfestival," celebrating the art of lace-making.
- The island of Capri, Italy, is known for its unique "Blue Grotto," a sea cave with blue luminescent waters.
- The Spanish town of Valencia is famous for its unique "Fallas" festival, where giant sculptures are displayed throughout the city and then ceremoniously burned.
- The British territory of Gibraltar is home to unique plant species, including the Gibraltar candytuft and the Gibraltar campion.
- The Estonian town of Türi hosts an annual "Türi Flower Festival," featuring elaborate flower displays and competitions.
- The city of Montpellier in France is home to the "Peyrou Promenade," a grand esplanade with a monumental water tower and stunning views.
- The Italian island of Procida is known for its pastel-colored houses and vibrant streets, making it a popular filming location for movies and TV shows.
- The country of Liechtenstein is one of the smallest countries in the world, with an area of just 160 square kilometers.
- The German town of Baden-Baden is famous for its thermal baths and spa culture, attracting visitors seeking relaxation and rejuvenation.
- The island of Menorca, Spain, is a UNESCO Biosphere Reserve, known for its unique natural beauty and diverse ecosystems.
- The Croatian town of Vis is known for its unique blue cave, where sunlight reflects off the white seabed to create a mesmerizing blue glow.
- The city of Debrecen in Hungary is famous for its annual "Flower Carnival," where participants create elaborate floral floats and costumes.

- The Scottish town of Stirling is home to the "Wallace Monument," a tower dedicated to the Scottish hero William Wallace.
- The island of Mallorca, Spain, is known for its unique breed of sheep, the "Mallorquina" sheep, used for their meat and wool.
- The French town of Eguisheim is known for its unique circular layout and is often considered one of the most beautiful villages in France.
- The city of Helsinki in Finland is famous for its unique architectural style known as "National Romanticism," featuring colorful buildings and intricate designs.
- The Estonian town of Viljandi is known for its unique "Viljandi Pärimusmuusika Festival," celebrating traditional Estonian folk music.
- The Italian island of Elba is famous for its unique flora, including several species of wild orchids.
- The British territory of Gibraltar has a unique breed of ape, the "Barbary macaque," the only wild monkey population in Europe.
- The island of Zakynthos in Greece is home to the "Navagio Beach," famous for its stunning shipwreck and crystal-clear waters.
- The Spanish town of Cuenca is known for its unique "Hanging Houses," perched on the edge of a steep cliff.
- The city of Gdańsk in Poland is famous for its unique architecture, combining elements of Gothic, Renaissance, and Baroque styles.
- The Norwegian town of Ålesund is known for its unique Art Nouveau architecture, with beautifully decorated buildings and facades.
- The Estonian town of Haapsalu is famous for its unique "Haapsalu Shawl," a traditional hand-knitted lace shawl.
- The British territory of Gibraltar is home to unique underground military tunnels, used during World War II and now open to the public as a historical attraction.
- The Finnish town of Savonlinna is famous for its annual "Savonlinna Opera Festival," held in the stunning medieval Olavinlinna Castle.
- The Romanian town of Sibiu is known for its unique "Eyes of Sibiu," small windows on the roofs of houses used for ventilation and to scare away evil spirits.

- The French town of Carcassonne is home to the "Cité de Carcassonne," a medieval fortress with impressive double walls and towers.
- The country of San Marino has its own unique set of postage stamps, showcasing the republic's cultural heritage.
- The Spanish island of Ibiza is famous for its unique nightlife and vibrant club scene, attracting partygoers from around the world.
- The Italian town of Castelluccio is famous for its "Fioritura," a unique natural phenomenon where fields of wildflowers bloom in vibrant colors.
- The Estonian town of Pärnu is known for its unique "Pärnu Mud Baths," where visitors can indulge in therapeutic mud treatments.
- The city of Jūrmala in Latvia is famous for its unique wooden architecture and beautiful sandy beaches.
- The German town of Badenweiler is known for its unique Roman baths and thermal springs, still used for relaxation and healing.
- The British territory of Gibraltar is home to the "Great Siege Tunnels," a network of tunnels and passages carved into the rock during the 18th century.
- The Scottish town of Portree on the Isle of Skye is known for its colorful houses and beautiful harbor.
- The French town of Collioure is famous for its unique light and vibrant colors, attracting many artists over the years.
- The Estonian town of Valga/Valka is unique because it shares its border with Latvia, and the main street acts as the international boundary.
- The Spanish city of Segovia is home to the "Aqueduct of Segovia," a well-preserved Roman aqueduct that still supplies water to the city.
- The Italian island of Pantelleria is known for its unique "dammusi," traditional domed stone houses with thick walls to withstand the heat.
- The Czech town of Hluboká nad Vltavou is famous for its picturesque Hluboká Castle, often referred to as the "Czech Windsor Castle."
- The British territory of Gibraltar is known for its unique "Gibraltar Candytuft," a small flowering plant found only in the region.

- The Finnish town of Naantali is famous for its "Moomin World," a theme park based on the beloved Moomin characters created by Tove Jansson.
- The Spanish town of Lugo is home to the "Roman Walls of Lugo," the best-preserved Roman walls in the world and a UNESCO World Heritage Site.
- The Italian island of Ischia is known for its unique "thermal parks," offering various spa treatments using the island's thermal waters.
- The Estonian town of Kuressaare is home to the "Bishop's Castle," one of the best-preserved medieval fortresses in the Baltic region.
- The city of Strasbourg in France is home to the "European Parliament," where representatives from EU member states meet to discuss and pass legislation.
- The British territory of Gibraltar has a unique system of red telephone boxes, similar to those in the United Kingdom.
- The Scottish town of Tobermory on the Isle of Mull is famous for its colorful buildings and scenic harbor.
- The French town of Bayeux is known for the "Bayeux Tapestry," a unique historical artwork depicting the Norman conquest of England.
- The Estonian town of Haanja is home to the unique "Suur Munamägi," the highest point in the Baltic states, offering stunning views from the observation tower.
- The Spanish town of Peñíscola is famous for its unique "Pope Luna Castle," used as a filming location for the TV series "Game of Thrones."
- The city of Ljubljana in Slovenia is known for its unique "Triple Bridge," a distinctive architectural feature connecting the historical and modern parts of the city.
- The Italian island of Procida is known for its unique "Corricella," a picturesque fishing village with colorful houses and narrow alleys.
- The British territory of Gibraltar is home to unique limestone formations called the "Apes' Den," where the Barbary macaques gather.
- The Romanian town of Sinaia is known for its beautiful "Peleş Castle," a neo-Renaissance castle once home to the Romanian royal family.

- The Finnish town of Porvoo is famous for its unique "Porvoo Doll and Toy Museum," displaying a vast collection of dolls and toys from different eras.
- The Spanish town of Zaragoza is home to the "Basilica of Our Lady of the Pillar," a famous pilgrimage site and a masterpiece of Baroque architecture.
- The Italian town of Gubbio is known for its unique "Corsa dei Ceri," a traditional race where participants carry large wooden structures through the town's narrow streets.
- The British territory of Gibraltar is famous for its unique "Gibraltar Barbary macaques," the only wild monkey population in Europe.
- The Estonian town of Tartu is home to the "Tartu Toy Museum," showcasing a diverse collection of toys from different periods and countries.
- The Scottish town of Melrose is known for its historic Melrose Abbey, a magnificent ruin with intricate carvings and a connection to the heart of Robert the Bruce.
- The French town of Le Mont-Saint-Michel is famous for its unique island commune and abbey, surrounded by breathtaking tidal waters.
- The German town of Lübeck is home to the "Holstentor," a well-preserved medieval city gate and a symbol of the city's history.
- The British territory of Gibraltar is known for its unique "Moorish Castle," a medieval fortress that offers panoramic views of the region.
- The Finnish town of Hämeenlinna is famous for its "Aulanko Nature Reserve," a lush forested area with beautiful walking trails and a stunning observation tower.
- The Spanish town of Ronda is known for its unique "Puente Nuevo," a striking bridge spanning a deep gorge.
- The Estonian town of Võru hosts an annual "Võru Folk Festival," celebrating Estonian folk music and dance.
- The Czech town of České Budějovice is famous for its unique "Black Tower," offering panoramic views of the city and the surrounding countryside.
- The Italian town of Orvieto is known for its unique "Orvieto Classico," a white wine produced from grapes grown on volcanic soil.
- The British territory of Gibraltar is home to the "Gibraltar Barb

- The Hungarian town of Eger is famous for its unique "Bull's Blood" wine, known for its dark red color and rich flavor.
- The Czech town of Telč is known for its unique "Telč Chateau," a stunning Renaissance-style castle surrounded by an ornamental lake.
- The Slovakian town of Banská Štiavnica is famous for its unique "Calvary," a religious complex with 25 chapels and three churches on a hilltop.
- The Polish city of Gdańsk is home to the "European Solidarity Center," a museum and cultural institution commemorating the history of the Solidarity movement.
- The Hungarian town of Pápa is known for its unique "Blue Dye Museum," dedicated to the history of indigo dyeing.
- The Romanian town of Sighişoara is famous for its unique "Saxons' Stairs," a covered wooden staircase with 176 steps leading up to the Church on the Hill.
- The Serbian town of Niš is home to the "Skull Tower," a unique monument built with human skulls after a battle during the First Serbian Uprising.
- The Lithuanian town of Biržai is known for its unique "Biržai Castle," a reconstructed castle surrounded by a defensive wall and moat.
- The Polish city of Wrocław is famous for its unique "Dwarfs of Wrocław," a collection of small bronze statues scattered throughout the city.
- The Ukrainian town of Chernobyl is known for the Chernobyl Nuclear Power Plant disaster, which occurred on April 26, 1986.
- The Hungarian town of Szeged is famous for its unique "Szeged Open-Air Festival," one of the largest outdoor theater events in Hungary.
- The Slovakian town of Bardejov is known for its unique "Bardejovské Kúpele," a spa resort with healing thermal waters.
- The Czech town of Kutná Hora is famous for its unique "Bone Church" or "Sedlec Ossuary," decorated with human bones.
- The Romanian town of Cluj-Napoca is home to the unique "Cluj-Napoca Botanical Garden," one of the largest in Eastern Europe.
- The Hungarian town of Debrecen is famous for its unique "Great Reformed Church," a stunning neoclassical church with an impressive 61-meter tall tower.

- The Polish town of Kalwaria Zebrzydowska is known for its unique "Kalwaria Zebrzydowska Sanctuary," a UNESCO World Heritage site with a series of chapels and shrines.
- The Serbian town of Subotica is famous for its unique "Subotica Synagogue," a beautiful art nouveau building, one of the largest synagogues in Europe.
- The Czech town of Karlovy Vary is known for its unique "Karlovy Vary International Film Festival," one of the oldest film festivals in the world.
- The Ukrainian town of Kamianets-Podilskyi is famous for its unique "Kamianets-Podilskyi Castle," situated on a rocky island in the middle of a river canyon.
- The Hungarian town of Eger is known for its unique "Valley of the Beautiful Women," a wine region with numerous wine cellars.
- The Polish city of Poznań is famous for its unique "Poznań International Fair," one of the oldest trade fairs in the world.
- The Croatian town of Varaždin is known for its unique "Varaždin Cemetery," a beautifully landscaped cemetery and one of the most significant in Croatia.
- The Slovakian town of Kežmarok is famous for its unique "Kežmarok Castle," a well-preserved Renaissance castle with stunning views of the High Tatras.
- The Hungarian town of Szentendre is known for its unique "Skanzen," an open-air ethnographic museum showcasing traditional Hungarian rural architecture.
- The Romanian town of Sibiu is famous for its unique "Astra National Museum Complex," one of the largest open-air museums in Europe.
- The Ukrainian city of Lviv is known for its unique "Lviv Opera House," an opulent neo-Renaissance theater that dates back to 1900.
- The Hungarian town of Keszthely is famous for its unique "Festetics Palace," one of the largest baroque castles in Hungary.
- The Polish city of Gdynia is known for its unique "Dar Pomorza," a tall ship used as a training vessel for the Polish Navy.
- The Croatian town of Trogir is famous for its unique "Trogir Cathedral," a stunning example of Romanesque and Gothic architecture.

- The Slovakian town of Košice is known for its unique "St. Elisabeth Cathedral," the largest church in Slovakia and a UNESCO World Heritage Site.
- The Romanian town of Timișoara is famous for its unique "Victory Square," known as the birthplace of the Romanian Revolution of 1989.
- The Hungarian town of Pécs is known for its unique "Early Christian Necropolis," a UNESCO World Heritage site with early Christian tombs and burial chambers.
- The Ukrainian town of Kamianets-Podilskyi is famous for its unique "Old Town," a well-preserved historic district with cobbled streets and medieval buildings.
- The Polish city of Bydgoszcz is known for its unique "Bydgoszcz Canal," an artificial waterway connecting the Vistula and Oder rivers.
- The Croatian town of Zadar is famous for its unique "Sea Organ," an architectural sound art installation that plays music using the movement of the sea.
- The Czech town of Škofja Loka is known for its unique "Škofja Loka Passion Play," one of the oldest plays of its kind in Central Europe.
- The Ukrainian city of Lviv is famous for its unique "Lviv High Castle," offering panoramic views of the city and the Carpathian Mountains.
- The Slovakian town of Trenčín is known for its unique "Trenčín Castle," a medieval fortress on a steep hill overlooking the town.
- The Romanian town of Sibiu is famous for its unique "Liars' Bridge," the first cast-iron bridge in Romania and known for its ornate decorations.
- The Hungarian town of Veszprém is known for its unique "Veszprém Zoo," one of the oldest zoos in Hungary.
- The Polish town of Zamość is famous for its unique "Zamość Syn
- The Czech town of Olomouc is known for its unique "Holy Trinity Column," a UNESCO World Heritage site and one of the largest Baroque sculptures in Europe.
- The Polish city of Lublin is famous for its unique "Lublin Castle," a medieval fortress with a distinctive round tower.

- The Slovakian town of Banská Bystrica is known for its unique "Banská Bystrica Fountain," the oldest urban fountain in Slovakia, dating back to the 16th century.
- The Hungarian town of Győr is famous for its unique "Győr National Theatre," one of the most modern theaters in Hungary.
- The Czech town of Česká Lípa is known for its unique "Česká Lípa Amphitheatre," an open-air theater carved into a sandstone rock.
- The Romanian town of Alba Iulia is famous for its unique "Alba Carolina Citadel," a star-shaped fortress and the largest of its kind in Romania.
- The Hungarian town of Debrecen is known for its unique "Nagyerdei Stadium," one of the largest stadiums in Hungary and the home of Debreceni VSC football club.
- The Polish city of Szczecin is famous for its unique "Szczecin Philharmonic Hall," a modern concert hall with a distinctive glass facade.
- The Slovakian town of Komárno is known for its unique "Fortress of Komárno," one of the largest fortification systems in Europe.
- The Hungarian town of Pécs is famous for its unique "Pécs University Library," featuring a modern architectural design.
- The Czech town of Kutná Hora is known for its unique "Hrádek," a medieval castle with a historical exhibition about the town's silver mining history.
- The Polish city of Toruń is famous for its unique "House Under the Star," a Gothic tenement house with a star-shaped facade.
- The Romanian town of Sibiu is known for its unique "Council Tower," offering panoramic views of the town and the surrounding Carpathian Mountains.
- The Hungarian town of Tatabánya is famous for its unique "Lake Medves," a former mine transformed into a recreational area with a lake and beach.
- The Czech town of Znojmo is known for its unique "Znojmo Catacombs," a labyrinth of underground passages and cellars.
- The Polish city of Gliwice is famous for its unique "Radio Tower Gliwice," a modernist radio broadcasting tower with a spiral staircase.
- The Romanian town of Cluj-Napoca is known for its unique "Cluj-Napoca Arena," one of the largest stadiums in Romania and the home of CFR Cluj football club.

- The Hungarian town of Szekszárd is famous for its unique "Szekszárd Wine Region," known for its red wines and traditional wine cellars.
- The Czech town of Litomyšl is known for its unique "Litomyšl Castle," a UNESCO World Heritage site and a Renaissance masterpiece.
- The Polish city of Kalisz is famous for its unique "Kaliszianka," a traditional folk dance performed by young girls in regional costumes.
- The Romanian town of Oradea is known for its unique "Moon Church," a stunning Baroque-style Catholic church with a unique clock face.
- The Hungarian town of Kecskemét is famous for its unique "Kecskemét Air Show," one of the largest air shows in Hungary.
- The Czech town of České Budějovice is known for its unique "České Budějovice Black Tower," offering panoramic views of the town and the surrounding countryside.
- The Polish city of Włocławek is famous for its unique "Włocławek Cathedral," a Gothic-style church with two asymmetrical towers.
- The Slovakian town of Žilina is known for its unique "Mariánska hora," a Marian pilgrimage site with a chapel and a large wooden cross.
- The Hungarian town of Nagykanizsa is famous for its unique "Nagykanizsa Theatre," a beautiful Neo-Renaissance building.
- The Romanian town of Sibiu is known for its unique "Potters' Tower," one of the nine original towers that still stand on the town's medieval walls.
- The Hungarian town of Eger is famous for its unique "Eger Castle," a historical fortress with a 16th-century minaret.
- The Czech town of Hradec Králové is known for its unique "White Tower," a historical observation tower offering views of the town.
- The Polish city of Bydgoszcz is famous for its unique "Bydgoszcz Canal Bridge," a movable bridge that connects two parts of the town.
- The Romanian town of Cluj-Napoca is known for its unique "Mikó Castle," a 16th-century Renaissance-style building.

- The Hungarian town of Pécs is famous for its unique "Vasarely Museum," dedicated to the works of Hungarian-born artist Victor Vasarely.
- The Polish city of Rzeszów is known for its unique "Podkarpackie Opera and Philharmonic," a modern cultural complex with a distinctive roof.
- The Romanian town of Brașov is famous for its unique "Black Church," the largest Gothic church in Romania.
- The Hungarian town of Szombathely is known for its unique "Iseum," a museum dedicated to the history of the cult of Isis in the Roman Empire.
- The Slovakian town of Poprad is famous for its unique "AquaCity Poprad," a thermal water park with numerous indoor and outdoor pools.
- The Czech town of Kutná Hora is known for its unique "St. Barbara's Church," a UNESCO World Heritage site and a masterpiece of Gothic architecture.
- The Polish city of Gorzów Wielkopolski is famous for its unique "Gorzów Palm House," a large greenhouse with tropical and subtropical plants.
- The Hungarian town of Eger is famous for its unique "Eger Thermal Bath," a complex of thermal pools and spa facilities.

Chapter 4: North America

- The Great Lakes in North America contain about 20% of the world's surface freshwater.
- Mexico City, the capital of Mexico, is built on top of an ancient lake.
- Canada has the world's longest coastline, stretching over 202,080 kilometers.
- The United States has the world's oldest living tree, a Bristlecone Pine in California estimated to be over 4,800 years old.
- The Chichen Itza pyramid in Mexico has a unique acoustic phenomenon - if you clap at the base, it echoes the sound of a Quetzal bird.
- The Bermuda Triangle, located in the western part of the North Atlantic Ocean, is famous for mysterious disappearances of ships and airplanes.
- The United States has a town called "Santa Claus" in Indiana.
- The Caribbean Sea is home to the deepest oceanic trench in the Atlantic, known as the "Puerto Rico Trench."
- The Niagara Falls between Canada and the United States is the largest waterfall in North America by volume.

- Mexico is the birthplace of chocolate, as the ancient Maya and Aztecs first cultivated cacao trees.
- The United States is home to the largest ball of twine, located in Cawker City, Kansas.
- The Bay of Fundy in Canada has the highest tidal range in the world, reaching up to 16.3 meters.
- Mexico's "Monarch Butterfly Biosphere Reserve" hosts millions of monarch butterflies during their migration.
- The United States is home to the "Hawaii Volcanoes National Park," showcasing two active volcanoes, Mauna Loa and Kilauea.
- The Baja California Peninsula in Mexico is the second-longest peninsula in the world, after the Arabian Peninsula.
- The Appalachian Mountains, stretching from Canada to Alabama, are one of the oldest mountain ranges on Earth.
- The United States and Canada share the world's longest international border, spanning over 8,891 kilometers.
- Mexico has a unique island called "Isla de las Munecas" (Island of the Dolls), covered in hundreds of creepy dolls hanging from trees.
- The United States is home to the world's oldest operating lighthouse, the "Boston Light," built in 1716.
- The highest point in North America is Denali (formerly known as Mount McKinley) in Alaska, standing at 6,190 meters.
- Canada has more lakes than all other countries combined, with an estimated 2 million lakes.
- The United States has a town called "Chicken" in Alaska and another called "Toad Suck" in Arkansas.
- The Mexican cuisine, known for its diverse flavors, was added to UNESCO's list of Intangible Cultural Heritage.
- Canada's name originates from the St. Lawrence Iroquoian word "kanata," meaning "village" or "settlement."
- The United States has a unique annual event called the "Running of the Bulls" in New Orleans, inspired by the Spanish tradition.
- The Yucatan Peninsula in Mexico was formed by a meteor impact over 65 million years ago, leading to the extinction of the dinosaurs.
- The United States has the world's first national park, Yellowstone National Park, established in 1872.

- Canada has the "Canadian Museum of Human Rights," the first museum solely dedicated to human rights.
- The United States has a town called "Lost Springs" in Wyoming, with a population of one person.
- The Mexican flag features an eagle perched on a cactus with a snake in its beak, inspired by an Aztec legend.
- The United States has a unique festival called "Burning Man" in Nevada's Black Rock Desert, known for its art installations and community spirit.
- Canada has the world's highest tides in the Bay of Fundy, reaching up to 16.3 meters.
- The United States has a unique natural landmark called the "Devils Tower," a massive volcanic formation in Wyoming.
- The "Mesoamerican Barrier Reef System" is the second-largest coral reef system in the world, extending along the coast of Mexico, Belize, Guatemala, and Honduras.
- The United States has a real town called "Hollywood" in California, famous for its film industry.
- Canada has a unique natural wonder called the "Hopewell Rocks," giant flowerpot-shaped rock formations exposed during low tide.
- The United States has a unique event called the "Running of the Reindeer" in Anchorage, Alaska, during the Fur Rendezvous Festival.
- The Mayan civilization, known for its advanced astronomy and mathematics, thrived in present-day Mexico, Guatemala, Honduras, El Salvador, and Belize.
- Canada has a unique island called "Pumpkin Island," which disappears underwater during high tide.
- The United States has a unique event called the "Cabbage Patch Baby Race" in Georgia, where participants race with baby dolls.
- Mexico is home to the "Sótano de las Golondrinas" (Cave of Swallows), a sinkhole with a depth of over 370 meters.
- The United States has a town called "Truth or Consequences" in New Mexico, named after a popular radio show.
- Canada has a unique underwater park called "Fathom Five National Marine Park," home to numerous shipwrecks and ancient rock formations.
- The United States has a town called "Intercourse" in Pennsylvania, named after a road intersection.

- Mexico's "Cave of Crystals" in Naica contains giant gypsum crystals, some measuring over 11 meters long.
- Canada's "Polar Bear Capital," Churchill, Manitoba, is famous for its polar bear population, attracting tourists from around the world.
- The United States is home to the world's largest ball of paint in Alexandria, Indiana, covered in over 25,000 layers of paint.
- Mexico's "Cenotes" are natural sinkholes filled with fresh groundwater, used by the ancient Maya for rituals and as water sources.
- The United States has a unique event called "La Tomatina" in Colorado, inspired by Spain's famous tomato-throwing festival.
- The Caribbean island of Saint Kitts and Nevis is the smallest country in the Americas in terms of both area and population.
- The United States has a town called "Bugtussle" in Kentucky, known for its quirky name.
- The Mayan city of Tikal in Guatemala is famous for its towering temples, including Temple IV, one of the tallest pre-Columbian structures in the Americas.
- The United States has a unique event called the "Cooper's Hill Cheese Rolling and Wake" in Gloucestershire, inspired by a traditional British event.
- The Caribbean island of Barbados is the birthplace of rum, with Mount Gay Distillery, established in 1703, being one of the oldest rum producers in the world.
- The Pacific Crest Trail, stretching over 4,270 kilometers, is a long-distance hiking trail that runs from Mexico to Canada through the United States.
- Mexico is the birthplace of the game "Championship Bull Riding," a popular rodeo sport.
- The United States has a unique event called "Frozen Dead Guy Days" in Colorado, featuring unconventional winter festivities.
- Canada's "Capilano Suspension Bridge" in British Columbia is a popular tourist attraction, allowing visitors to cross a deep canyon.
- The United States has a town called "Funkstown" in Maryland, known for its musical name.
- The Caribbean island of Dominica is home to the world's second-largest hot spring, Boiling Lake, known for its bubbling and steaming water.

- The United States has a unique event called the "Iditarod Trail Sled Dog Race" in Alaska, one of the toughest sled dog races in the world.
- Mexico's "Grutas de Cacahuamilpa National Park" contains extensive cave systems with impressive stalactites and stalagmites.
- The United States has a town called "Idiotville" in Oregon, known for its peculiar name.
- Canada's "Gros Morne National Park" in Newfoundland and Labrador is a UNESCO World Heritage site, featuring dramatic fjords and diverse landscapes.
- The United States has a unique event called "Frozen Dead Guy Days" in Colorado, featuring unconventional winter festivities.
- Mexico's "Grutas de Cacahuamilpa National Park" contains extensive cave systems with impressive stalactites and stalagmites.
- The United States has a town called "Idiotville" in Oregon, known for its peculiar name.
- Canada's "Gros Morne National Park" in Newfoundland and Labrador is a UNESCO World Heritage site, featuring dramatic fjords and diverse landscapes.
- The United States has a unique event called the "Mullet Toss" in Florida, where participants throw mullet fish across state lines for fun.
- The United States has a town called "Uncertain" in Texas, with a name as uncertain as its origin.
- Canada's "Bay of Fundy" is known for having the highest tidal range in the world, creating the "Tidal Bore," a wave that travels up rivers.
- The United States has a unique event called the "Cheese Rolling and Wake" in Gloucestershire, inspired by a traditional British event.
- The "Mayan Ruins of Tulum" in Mexico are perched on a cliff overlooking the Caribbean Sea, providing stunning views.
- Canada's "Dinosaur Provincial Park" in Alberta is a UNESCO World Heritage site, containing an abundance of dinosaur fossils.
- The United States has a unique event called "International Water Tasting" in West Virginia, where participants taste and judge different types of water.

- Mexico's "Hierve el Agua" is a petrified waterfall formed by mineral-rich spring waters over thousands of years.
- The United States has a town called "Monowi" in Nebraska, known for having a population of one person.
- Canada's "Hopewell Rocks" in New Brunswick are famous for their flowerpot-shaped rock formations caused by tidal erosion.
- The United States has a unique event called "La Tomatina" in Colorado, inspired by Spain's famous tomato-throwing festival.
- Mexico is home to the "Great Pyramid of Cholula," the largest pyramid in terms of volume, surpassing even the Great Pyramid of Giza.
- Canada's "Yoho National Park" in British Columbia features stunning waterfalls, soaring peaks, and the famous Burgess Shale fossil beds.
- The United States has a unique event called "The Burning of Zozobra" in New Mexico, a tradition to banish worries and troubles.
- Mexico's "Palacio de Bellas Artes" in Mexico City is a grand arts center and opera house featuring stunning murals and exhibitions.
- The United States has a town called "Santa Claus" in Indiana.
- Canada's "Nahanni National Park Reserve" in the Northwest Territories contains deep canyons and stunning waterfalls, including the impressive Virginia Falls.
- The United States has a unique event called the "Ostrich Festival" in Arizona, featuring ostrich races and various entertainment.
- Mexico's "Cave of Crystals" in Naica contains giant gypsum crystals, some measuring over 11 meters long.
- The United States has a town called "Truth or Consequences" in New Mexico, named after a popular radio show.
- The Caribbean island of Jamaica is the birthplace of reggae music, with legendary musician Bob Marley hailing from the island.
- The United States has a town called "Cut and Shoot" in Texas, known for its peculiar name and origin.
- Canada's "Waterton Lakes National Park" in Alberta shares a border with Glacier National Park in the United States, forming the world's first international peace park.

- The United States has a unique event called "Avocado Festival" in California, celebrating the love for avocados with various avocado-themed activities.
- Mexico's "Museo Nacional de Antropología" in Mexico City is one of the world's largest and most comprehensive museums dedicated to anthropology.
- The United States has a town called "French Lick" in Indiana, known for its unusual name and historic mineral springs.
- The largest Pacific island in North America is Vancouver, in British Columbia, Canada.
- The United States has a unique event called the "Calf Fry" in Oklahoma, a festival featuring live country music and various calf-related activities.
- Mexico is home to the "Teotihuacan," an ancient Mesoamerican city with the massive Pyramid of the Sun and the Pyramid of the Moon.
- The United States has a town called "Muleshoe" in Texas, known for its quirky name.
- Canada's "Magnetic Hill" in New Brunswick is an optical illusion where cars appear to roll uphill due to the surrounding landscape.
- The United States has a unique event called "Frozen Dead Guy Days" in Colorado, featuring unconventional winter festivities.
- Mexico's "Copper Canyon" is a network of canyons larger and deeper than the Grand Canyon in the United States.
- The United States has a town called "Noodle" in Texas, known for its noodle-related name.
- Canada's "Montmorency Falls" in Quebec are taller than Niagara Falls, reaching up to 84 meters.
- The United States has a unique event called the "O. Henry Pun-Off" in Texas, featuring a pun competition.
- Mexico's "Museo Subacuático de Arte" (Underwater Museum of Art) in Cancún displays underwater sculptures, combining art with marine conservation.
- Canada's "Head-Smashed-In Buffalo Jump" in Alberta is a UNESCO World Heritage site, preserving a traditional hunting method used by Indigenous peoples.
- The United States has a unique event called "Great American Duck Race" in New Mexico, featuring racing ducks and various festivities.

- Mexico's "Guanajuato Mummy Museum" houses naturally mummified bodies discovered in a local cemetery.
- The United States has a town called "Boring" in Oregon, known for its amusingly dull name.
- Canada's "Rideau Canal" in Ontario is the oldest continuously operated canal system in North America.
- The United States has a unique event called the "Cassville Turkey Trot" in Missouri, featuring a race with live turkeys.
- Mexico's "Chapultepec Castle" in Mexico City was once the residence of Emperor Maximilian I and Empress Carlota.
- Canada's "Haida Gwaii" (formerly Queen Charlotte Islands) in British Columbia is known for its rich Indigenous culture and totem poles.
- The United States has a unique event called "Cabbage Night" in New England, where teenagers play pranks the night before Halloween.
- Mexico's "Cenotes" are natural sinkholes filled with fresh groundwater, used by the ancient Maya for rituals and as water sources.
- The United States has a town called "Santa Claus" in Indiana.
- Canada's "Bay of Fundy" is known for having the highest tidal range in the world, creating the "Tidal Bore," a wave that travels up rivers.
- The United States has a unique event called the "Cooper's Hill Cheese Rolling and Wake" in Gloucestershire, inspired by a traditional British event.
- Mexico's "Hierve el Agua" is a petrified waterfall formed by mineral-rich spring waters over thousands of years.
- Canada's "Gros Morne National Park" in Newfoundland and Labrador is a UNESCO World Heritage site, featuring dramatic fjords and diverse landscapes.
- Mexico's "Grutas de Cacahuamilpa National Park" contains extensive cave systems with impressive stalactites and stalagmites.
- The United States has a town called "Idiotville" in Oregon, known for its peculiar name.
- Canada's "Magnetic Hill" in New Brunswick is an optical illusion where cars appear to roll uphill due to the surrounding landscape.
- The United States has a town called "Zzyzx" in California, known for having the last word in the English language.

- Canada's "Cathedral Grove" on Vancouver Island is home to ancient Douglas fir and red cedar trees, some over 800 years old.
- The United States has a unique event called "Great Texas Mosquito Festival" in Texas, celebrating the pesky insect with games and contests.
- Mexico's "Xochimilco" is famous for its floating gardens and colorful trajineras, traditional boats used for tours on the canals.
- The United States has a town called "Superior" in Arizona, known for its misleadingly ordinary name.
- Canada's "Kluane National Park" in Yukon contains the largest non-polar ice fields in the world.
- The United States has a unique event called the "Stinking Rose Festival" in California, celebrating all things garlic.
- Mexico's "Museo Nacional del Virreinato" in Tepotzotlán showcases art and history from the Spanish colonial era.
- The United States has a town called "What Cheer" in Iowa, known for its curious name with an upbeat message.
- Canada's "Fossil Forest" in Joggins, Nova Scotia, is a UNESCO World Heritage site with well-preserved fossils from the Carboniferous period.
- The United States has a unique event called the "Ostrich Festival" in Arizona, featuring ostrich races and various entertainment.
- Mexico's "Jardin Botanico de Vallarta" (Vallarta Botanical Gardens) in Puerto Vallarta showcases diverse plant species in a beautiful natural setting.
- The United States has a town called "Fiddletown" in California, named after a fiddle-playing gold prospector.
- Canada's "Whistler Blackcomb" in British Columbia is one of the largest ski resorts in North America.
- The United States has a unique event called the "Cow Chip Throwing Capital of the World Championship" in Kansas, where participants throw cow chips (dried cow dung).
- Mexico's "Tequila" in Jalisco is the birthplace of tequila, a distilled alcoholic beverage made from the blue agave plant.
- The United States has a town called "Zap" in North Dakota, known for its snappy name.
- Canada's "Niagara-on-the-Lake" in Ontario is famous for its wineries and the Shaw Festival, a renowned theater event.

- The United States has a unique event called "Punkin Chunkin" in Delaware, where participants launch pumpkins using various contraptions.
- Canada's "Casa Loma" in Toronto is a majestic castle-like mansion, serving as a popular tourist attraction and event venue.
- The United States has a unique event called the "Coconut Grove Bed Race" in Florida, featuring creatively decorated beds on wheels racing through the streets.
- Mexico's "Sumidero Canyon" in Chiapas features towering cliffs and a river flowing through its depths.
- The United States has a town called "Hell" in Michigan, known for its tongue-in-cheek tourism promotions.
- Canada's "Vieux-Québec" (Old Quebec) in Quebec City is a UNESCO World Heritage site, featuring charming cobblestone streets and historic architecture.
- Mexico's "Xel-Há Park" on the Riviera Maya offers a natural aquatic playground for snorkeling and swimming.
- The United States has a town called "Earth" in Texas, residing on solid ground.
- Canada's "Jellybean Row" in St. John's, Newfoundland, features colorful row houses along the city streets.
- The United States has a unique event called the "Texas Cowboy Poetry Gathering" in Texas, celebrating the cowboy tradition through poetry and storytelling.
- Mexico's "Palenque" is a famous archaeological site showcasing the stunning Temple of the Inscriptions.
- The United States has a town called "Normal" in Illinois, known for being anything but ordinary.
- Canada's "Cabot Trail" in Nova Scotia offers breathtaking views along a scenic drive through the Cape Breton Highlands.
- The United States has a unique event called "National Hollerin' Contest" in North Carolina, where participants compete in hollering (loud vocalizations).
- Mexico's "Cabo Pulmo National Park" in Baja California Sur is a marine sanctuary with a diverse array of sea life.
- The United States has a town called "Sleepy Hollow" in New York, known for its connection to the famous Washington Irving tale.
- Canada's "Athabasca Sand Dunes Provincial Park" in Saskatchewan is home to the largest active sand dunes in North America.

- The United States has a unique event called the "Great Fruitcake Toss" in Colorado, where participants throw fruitcakes as far as they can.
- Mexico's "Palacio de Gobierno" in Mexico City features Diego Rivera's famous murals depicting Mexico's history.
- The United States has a town called "Gnaw Bone" in Indiana, with a name that might make you hungry.
- Canada's "Sainte-Anne-de-Bellevue Canal" in Quebec is the oldest canal in North America, still in operation.
- The United States has a unique event called "Mud Day" in Michigan, where participants get messy in a massive mud pit.
- The United States has a town called "Slaughterville" in Oklahoma, with a name that may raise some eyebrows.
- Canada's "Baffin Island" in Nunavut is the fifth-largest island in the world and home to a diverse Arctic landscape.
- Mexico's "Paricutín Volcano" in Michoacán is the youngest volcano in North America, formed in 1943.
- The United States has a town called "Dinosaur" in Colorado, a fitting location for any dinosaur enthusiasts.
- Canada's "Rideau Canal" in Ontario becomes the world's largest skating rink during the winter, offering a unique ice-skating experience.
- The United States has a unique event called the "Albuquerque International Balloon Fiesta" in New Mexico, featuring hundreds of colorful hot air balloons taking flight.
- Mexico's "Casa Azul" (Blue House) in Mexico City was the home of artist Frida Kahlo and is now a museum dedicated to her life and works.
- The United States has a town called "Embarrass" in Minnesota, known for its frigidly ironic name.
- Canada's "Joggins Fossil Cliffs" in Nova Scotia provide a window into the ancient past, with well-preserved fossils from the "Coal Age."
- The United States has a unique event called the "Coney Island Mermaid Parade" in New York, celebrating sea-themed costumes and creativity.
- Mexico's "Cañón del Sumidero" in Chiapas features towering cliffs and a river flowing through its depths.
- The United States has a town called "Cool" in California, where residents enjoy a chill atmosphere.

- Canada's "Royal Tyrrell Museum" in Alberta houses one of the world's largest displays of dinosaur fossils.
- The United States has a unique event called "Lawnmower Racing" in Illinois, where souped-up lawnmowers race for glory.
- Mexico's "Museo Nacional de Arte" (National Museum of Art) in Mexico City displays an extensive collection of Mexican art from the colonial period to the present.
- The United States has a town called "Dime Box" in Texas, known for its intriguingly small-town name.
- Canada's "Whale Interpretive Centre" in British Columbia educates visitors about the region's marine life and conservation efforts.
- Mexico's "Huatulco National Park" in Oaxaca protects a biodiverse coastal area with lush rainforests and pristine beaches.
- The United States has a town called "Nameless" in Tennessee, with a name that speaks for itself.
- Canada's "Kejimkujik National Park" in Nova Scotia is a designated Dark Sky Preserve, offering exceptional stargazing opportunities.
- The United States has a unique event called the "World Championship of Frog Jumping" in California, inspired by Mark Twain's short story.
- Mexico's "Parque Ecológico Chipinque" in Nuevo León provides scenic hiking trails and panoramic views of Monterrey.
- The United States has a town called "Goobertown" in Arkansas, known for its whimsical name.
- The United States has a unique event called the "Calf Fry" in Oklahoma, a festival featuring live country music and various calf-related activities.
- The United States has a town called "Zap" in North Dakota, known for its snappy name.
- Canada's "Niagara-on-the-Lake" in Ontario is famous for its wineries and the Shaw Festival, a renowned theater event.
- In Canada, there is a small town called "Sourtoe," known for its famous tradition of serving drinks with a real human toe inside.
- The United States' official national gemstone is the "opal," which symbolizes hope and purity.
- In Mexico, there is a town called "Chihuahua," which is also the name of the smallest dog breed in the world.

- The United States' longest-running TV show is "Meet the Press," a weekly political talk show that has been airing since 1947.
- Canada's "Dildo Run Provincial Park" in Newfoundland and Labrador is known for its unique and giggle-inducing name.
- The "Jackalope" is a mythical creature of North American folklore, believed to be a cross between a jackrabbit and an antelope.
- In Mexico, you can find a town called "Mexicali," famous for its heat, as it ranks among the hottest cities in the world.
- Canada's "Festival du Voyageur" in Manitoba celebrates French-Canadian culture and history with music, dancing, and snow sculptures.
- The "Chiricahua leopard frog" is an amphibian species native to the southwestern United States and northern Mexico.
- In the United States, there is a museum called the "Museum of Bad Art," dedicated to showcasing exceptionally bad art pieces.
- Canada's Yukon territory is home to the "Signpost Forest" in Watson Lake, where visitors can leave their own signposts with messages from all over the world.
- In Mexico, there is a town called "Santa Claus" in the state of Chihuahua, which often receives thousands of letters addressed to Santa Claus from children around the world.
- The United States' state of Pennsylvania is home to the "Hershey's Chocolate World," a fun and interactive chocolate-themed attraction.
- In Canada, there is a small village called "Saint-Louis-du-Ha! Ha!," known for its quirky name with repeated laughter.
- The "Mexican walking fish," also known as the axolotl, is a unique aquatic salamander that can regenerate lost limbs.
- In the United States, the "Seattle Gum Wall" is a peculiar tourist attraction where visitors stick chewing gum on the walls of an alley.
- Canada's province of Newfoundland and Labrador is home to the "Moose Capital of the World," with a large population of these majestic animals.
- The "Rusty patched bumblebee" is an endangered species found in the United States and Canada.
- In Mexico, there is a small town called "Villa Corona," which means "Crown Town" in English, with a unique name.

- The United States' state of Wyoming is home to the "Jackalope" statue, a symbol of quirky American folklore.
- Canada's province of Ontario is home to the "Narwhal," a fascinating Arctic whale species known for its long, spiral tusk.
- The "Sonora Desert toad," found in the southwestern United States and Mexico, secretes a potent psychedelic substance known as "bufotoxin."
- In the United States, there is a town called "Boring" in Oregon, which has a sister city named "Dull" in Scotland.
- Canada's city of Winnipeg in Manitoba is known for its "Festival of Fools," where participants dress in silly costumes and participate in humorous events.
- The "Grizzly bear" is a powerful mammal found in various regions of North America, known for its size and strength.
- In Mexico, there is a town called "Tierra Blanca," which means "White Land" in English, with a seemingly straightforward name.
- The United States' state of Alaska is home to the "Moose Dropping Festival," where participants play games with moose droppings.
- Canada's "Capilano Suspension Bridge" in British Columbia has a quirky attraction called the "Cliffwalk," a narrow walkway along the cliffs.
- The "American burying beetle" is an endangered species found in parts of the United States and Canada, known for its unique burial behavior.
- In Mexico, there is a town called "Buenos Aires," which means "Good Air" in English, with a pleasant name. Buenos Aires is also the name of the capital of Argentina.
- The United States' state of Montana is home to the "Testicle Festival," a unique event centered around consuming deep-fried bull testicles.
- The United States' state of Oregon is home to a unique attraction called "The Oregon Vortex," known for its optical illusions and gravity-defying phenomena.
- In Canada, there is a town called "Ding Dong" in Newfoundland and Labrador, known for its whimsical name.
- The "Quokka" is a small marsupial found in Australia, but it is also sometimes referred to as the "happiest animal in the world."

- In Mexico, there is a town called "El Tule," home to the "El Árbol del Tule," the world's stoutest tree, with a circumference of over 137 feet.
- Canada's "Cabbagetown" in Toronto is a historic neighborhood with a peculiar name derived from its early residents' habit of growing cabbages in their front yards.
- The United States' state of Arizona is home to the "London Bridge" in Lake Havasu City, brought over from London and reassembled brick by brick.
- In Mexico, there is a town called "Los Mochis," which translates to "The Saps" in English, with an amusing name.
- The "Horned lizard" found in the southwestern United States and Mexico can shoot blood from its eyes as a defense mechanism.
- In the United States, there is a town called "Looneyville" in West Virginia, known for its humorous name.
- Canada's "Enchanted Forest" in British Columbia is a theme park featuring fairy tale characters and whimsical sculptures.
- The United States' state of South Dakota is home to "Wall Drug," a quirky roadside attraction that offers free ice water to travelers.
- In the United States, there is a town called "Hazard" in Kentucky, known for its ironically named welcome sign that reads "Welcome to Hazard, KY - It's a Good Place to Live."
- Canada's "Grosse Île" in Quebec was once a quarantine station for immigrants arriving in Canada during the 19th and early 20th centuries.
- The United States' state of California is home to the "Winchester Mystery House," a peculiar mansion filled with staircases that lead to nowhere and secret passages.
- In Mexico, there is a town called "Pantepec," which means "Place of Bats" in English, with a name that might conjure images of winged creatures.
- The "Nine-banded armadillo" is an interesting creature found in the southern United States and parts of Mexico, known for rolling into a ball as a defense mechanism.
- In Canada, there is a town called "Kleena Kleene" in British Columbia, known for its charmingly repetitive name.
- The United States' state of Nevada is home to the "International Banana Museum," featuring a vast collection of banana-themed memorabilia.

- Canada's "Casa Loma" in Toronto is a grand castle-like mansion, rumored to be haunted by the ghost of its former owner.
- In Mexico, there is a town called "Taxco," famous for its silver mining and exquisite silver jewelry.
- The "American woodcock" is a bird found in eastern North America, known for its elaborate and mesmerizing courtship display.
- Canada's "Icefields Parkway" in Alberta offers stunning views of glaciers, waterfalls, and turquoise lakes, making it one of the most beautiful drives in the world.
- The United States' state of Utah is home to the "Bonneville Salt Flats," where land-speed records have been set due to the flat and salty terrain.
- In Mexico, there is a town called "Cuitzeo," which means "Place of Snakes" in English, with a name that might send shivers down your spine.
- The "Hoatzin" is a peculiar bird found in South America but is often referred to as the "stink bird" due to its unpleasant smell.
- Canada's "Enchanted Forest" in British Columbia is a theme park featuring fairy tale characters and whimsical sculptures.
- The United States' state of South Dakota is home to "Wall Drug," a quirky roadside attraction that offers free ice water to travelers.
- The "Nine-banded armadillo" is an interesting creature found in the southern United States and parts of Mexico, known for rolling into a ball as a defense mechanism.
- Canada's "Casa Loma" in Toronto is a grand castle-like mansion, rumored to be haunted by the ghost of its former owner.
- In Mexico, there is a town called "Taxco," famous for its silver mining and exquisite silver jewelry.
- The "American woodcock" is a bird found in eastern North America, known for its elaborate and mesmerizing courtship display.
- The "Three-toed sloth" found in Central and South America is known for its slow and deliberate movements, spending most of its life hanging upside down from trees.
- In Mexico, there is a town called "Mazamitla," which means "Place of Deer" in English, with a name that connects it to its natural surroundings.

- Canada's "Medicine Hat" in Alberta is known for the "Saamis Tepee," the world's tallest tepee-shaped structure.
- The United States' state of Utah is home to "Goblin Valley State Park," where unique rock formations known as "hoodoos" resemble goblins.
- In Mexico, there is a town called "Cuernavaca," which means "Place of Ears" in English, with a name that may prompt curiosity.
- The "Coati" is a raccoon-like animal found in North, Central, and South America, known for its long snout and playful behavior.
- Canada's "Head-Smashed-In Buffalo Jump" in Alberta is a UNESCO World Heritage site, preserving a historic buffalo hunting site used by indigenous people.
- The United States' state of Oklahoma is home to a museum dedicated to "Pops," a quirky gas station and soda pop store featuring a giant soda bottle sculpture.
- In Mexico, there is a town called "Tula," known for its ancient archaeological site with impressive stone warrior sculptures.
- Canada's "Tungsten City" in Northwest Territories was once a bustling mining town but is now a ghost town with eerie remnants of its past.
- The United States' state of Colorado is home to the "Shrine of the Sun," a unique underground chapel and museum built inside a mountain.
- In Mexico, there is a town called "Villahermosa," which means "Beautiful Town" in English, with a name that reflects its charm.
- In the United States, there is a town called "It's a Long Drive" in Texas, known for its name that probably requires a long drive to reach.
- Canada's "Lost Lake" in British Columbia mysteriously disappears during the summer months, only to reappear in the winter.
- The United States' state of Kentucky is home to the "Wigwam Village Motel," featuring vintage wigwam-shaped cabins for lodging.
- In Mexico, there is a town called "Sahagún," named after a Spanish monk and known for its historical significance.

- Canada's "Old Quebec Funicular" in Quebec City is a unique inclined railway that connects the lower town with the upper town.
- The United States' state of Oregon is home to the "Lavender Daze Festival," a celebration of all things lavender with unique lavender products and displays.
- In Mexico, there is a town called "Matamoros," named after a Mexican independence hero, but its name translates to "Killer of Moors" in English.
- Canada's "Prince Edward Island" is known for its "Potato Blossom Festival," celebrating the island's famous potatoes.
- The United States' state of Nevada is home to the "Museum of Neon Art," featuring a collection of neon signs and art.
- In Mexico, there is a town called "Lerdo," which means "Slow" in English, with a humorous name.
- Canada's "Hell's Gate Airtram" in British Columbia offers a thrilling ride over the Fraser River canyon.
- The United States' state of Florida is home to "The Citrus Tower," a unique observation tower that once offered panoramic views of orange groves.
- In Mexico, there is a town called "Ascension," meaning "Ascension" in English, with a name that suggests elevation.
- Canada's "World's Largest Hockey Stick" in British Columbia stands at over 60 meters tall, celebrating the country's love for hockey.
- The United States' state of Utah is home to a unique "Hole N' The Rock" attraction, a home carved into a massive rock formation.
- In Mexico, there is a town called "Ángel R. Cabada," named after a Mexican politician, with an angelic name.
- Canada's "Mad Trapper" in Yukon was a mysterious fugitive who led authorities on a famous manhunt in the early 1900s.
- The United States' state of Colorado is home to the "National Museum of Roller Skating," celebrating the history and culture of roller skating.
- In Mexico, there is a town called "Epitacio Huerta," named after a Mexican general and politician, with an impressive name.
- The United States' state of California is home to a unique attraction called "The Museum of Jurassic Technology," a blend of art and science with eccentric exhibits.

- In Mexico, there is a town called "Frontera," which means "Border" in English, with a name that suggests a geographical significance.
- Canada's "Polar Bear Jail" in Churchill, Manitoba, is used to temporarily house polar bears that wander into town until they can be safely relocated.
- The United States' state of New York is home to the "Big Duck," a peculiar building shaped like a giant duck.
- In Mexico, there is a town called "Nada," which means "Nothing" in English, with a name that might raise eyebrows.
- Canada's "The Keg Mansion" in Toronto is a historic restaurant housed in a mansion once owned by the founder of Canada's Dominion Bank.
- The United States' state of Nevada is home to the "International Car Forest of the Last Church," an art installation featuring cars buried nose-first in the ground.
- In Mexico, there is a town called "Miracle," known for its intriguingly optimistic name.
- Canada's "Lytton" in British Columbia is often recognized as the "Hot Spot of Canada," with the highest recorded temperature in the country.

Chapter 5: South America

- South America is the fourth-largest continent, covering an area of about 17.8 million square kilometers.
- The Amazon Rainforest, located in South America, is the largest tropical rainforest in the world.
- The Amazon River, also in South America, is the second-longest river globally, after the Nile.
- The highest waterfall in the world, Angel Falls, is situated in Venezuela, South America, with a height of 979 meters (3,212 feet).
- South America is home to the world's highest navigable lake, Lake Titicaca, located between Bolivia and Peru.
- The driest desert on Earth, the Atacama Desert, is found in Chile, South America.
- The Andes, the longest mountain range in the world, runs along the western edge of South America.
- The official language of Brazil, the largest country in South America, is Portuguese.

- The national dance of Argentina is the tango, known for its passionate and dramatic moves.
- The Galápagos Islands, off the coast of Ecuador, played a significant role in Charles Darwin's development of the theory of evolution.
- In Colombia, there is a city named "Santa Cruz del Islote," located on a tiny, densely populated artificial island.
- Venezuela has the world's highest waterfall, Angel Falls, which drops uninterrupted from a height of 979 meters (3,212 feet).
- Suriname is the smallest country in South America, covering an area of approximately 163,821 square kilometers.
- The traditional music of the Andes, played on panpipes and drums, is called "Andean folk music" or "Andean panpipe music."
- The "Inca Trail" in Peru is a famous hiking route that leads to the ancient city of Machu Picchu.
- South America has the largest variety of parrot species in the world.
- The largest salt flat in the world, the Salar de Uyuni, is located in Bolivia.
- In Brazil, there is an island named "Ilha da Queimada Grande," also known as "Snake Island," where a large population of venomous snakes lives.
- Ecuador is the only country in the world named after a geographical feature, the equator.
- The "Guanaco" is a wild, llama-like animal found in the highlands of South America.
- The "Uros" people of Peru live on floating islands made of reeds in Lake Titicaca.
- The "Teatro Amazonas" in Manaus, Brazil, is an opera house located deep in the Amazon Rainforest.
- In Chile, there is a valley called "Valle de la Luna" or "Valley of the Moon," known for its lunar-like landscape.
- Colombia is one of the world's leading producers of emeralds.
- The "Christ the Redeemer" statue in Rio de Janeiro, Brazil, is one of the New Seven Wonders of the World.
- The official currency of Argentina is the "Argentine Peso."
- The "Easter Island" (Rapa Nui) in Chile is famous for its mysterious and enormous stone statues called "moai."
- The "Páramo" is a unique high-altitude ecosystem found in the Andes, known for its diverse plant and animal life.

- Peru is home to the highest sand dune in the world, known as "Cerro Blanco."
- The "Tepui" are flat-topped mountains found mainly in Venezuela and Guyana.
- The national dance of Uruguay is called the "Candombe," influenced by African rhythms.
- The "Carretera Austral" is a remote highway that stretches through the stunning landscapes of Chilean Patagonia.
- The "Carnaval" celebration in Brazil is one of the biggest and most vibrant festivals in the world.
- The "Angelito" dance of Bolivia features dancers balancing a bottle of wine on their heads.
- "Pablo Escobar" was one of the most notorious drug lords in history and operated from Colombia.
- The "Perito Moreno Glacier" in Argentina is one of the few glaciers in the world that is advancing instead of retreating.
- The "Jesuit Missions" in Paraguay are UNESCO World Heritage Sites, showcasing the Jesuits' historical architectural work.
- The "Salt Cathedral of Zipaquirá" in Colombia is an underground Roman Catholic church built within a salt mine.
- The "Capuchin Catacombs" in Colombia house mummified bodies displayed in glass cabinets.
- Brazil is the largest producer of coffee in the world.
- The "Nazca Lines" in Peru are ancient geoglyphs etched into the desert floor, visible only from the air.
- In "Villa Epecuén," Argentina, there is a town that was submerged underwater for 25 years and re-emerged in 2009.
- The "Galápagos Tortoise" can live up to 100 years or more, making it one of the longest-lived reptiles.
- "Rurrenabaque," Bolivia, is known for its "Yungas Road," often called the "World's Most Dangerous Road" due to its treacherous conditions.
- The "Lençóis Maranhenses National Park" in Brazil features stunning white sand dunes dotted with rainwater lagoons.
- The "Río Tinto" in the Atacama Desert of Chile has water that appears reddish due to iron content, earning it the name "Red River."
- The "Boca Juniors" and "River Plate" soccer teams in Argentina have one of the most intense rivalries in the world of football.

- Guyana is the only South American country where English is the official language.
- The "Pink Dolphin," also known as the "Amazon River Dolphin," is found in the Amazon River basin.
- The "Tiwanaku" civilization in Bolivia predates the Inca Empire and is renowned for its advanced engineering and architecture.
- The "Angel's Trumpet" flower, found in South America, is known for its large, trumpet-shaped blooms and potent hallucinogenic properties.
- The "Llanos" is a vast grassy plain in Venezuela and Colombia, known for its seasonal flooding and rich biodiversity.
- The "Galápagos Islands" are a volcanic archipelago known for inspiring Charles Darwin's theory of natural selection.
- The "Darién Gap" is a dense and impassable rainforest that separates Panama from Colombia, making it one of the few missing links in the Pan-American Highway.
- The "Urus" people of Bolivia are known for their ancient tradition of building floating islands made of totora reeds on Lake Titicaca.
- South America has the world's largest river, the Amazon River, which discharges more water than the next seven largest rivers combined.
- In "Pantanal," Brazil, the largest wetland on Earth, there are thousands of caimans living in harmony with other wildlife.
- The "El Tatio" geyser field in Chile is the highest geyser field in the world.
- The "El Salvador Mine" in Chile is one of the largest open-pit copper mines globally, visible even from space.
- The "Calbuco" volcano in Chile erupted twice in 2015 after being dormant for over 40 years.
- The "Cerro Rico" in Bolivia, also known as the "Mountain that Eats Men," was one of the richest sources of silver during colonial times.
- "Roraima" is a massive flat-topped mountain located at the triple border of Venezuela, Brazil, and Guyana, inspiring Sir Arthur Conan Doyle's novel "The Lost World."
- The "Nazca Lines" in Peru include over 300 geoglyphs depicting various animals, plants, and geometric shapes.
- The "Misti" volcano in Peru is considered one of the most dangerous volcanoes in South America due to its proximity to the city of Arequipa.

- In "Rio de Janeiro," Brazil, there is a "Selarón Steps," a vibrant and colorful staircase covered in mosaic tiles from over 60 countries.
- The "Mato Grosso" region in Brazil is known for its abundant wildlife and is one of the best places in the world to spot jaguars in the wild.
- The "Atacama Desert" in Chile is often used as a Mars analogue for testing rovers and conducting research on extremophiles.
- "Easter Island" statues, called "moai," were carved from volcanic rock by the Rapa Nui people between 1250 and 1500 CE.
- The "Iguazu Falls" at the border of Argentina and Brazil is one of the most stunning waterfalls in the world, with over 270 cascades.
- The "Cerro Paranal Observatory" in Chile houses some of the world's most advanced telescopes for observing the universe.
- "Peru" is home to over 3,000 varieties of potatoes, making it a vital center of potato diversity.
- The "Piedras Rojas" (Red Stones) in Chile are striking red rock formations surrounded by a salt flat.
- "Cuy" (guinea pig) is a traditional delicacy in Peru and Ecuador.
- The "Cristo de la Concordia" in Bolivia is a statue of Christ that is taller than the iconic "Christ the Redeemer" statue in Rio de Janeiro.
- The "Pululahua Geobotanical Reserve" in Ecuador is located within a volcanic crater and is one of the only inhabited volcanic calderas worldwide.
- In "La Paz," Bolivia, there is a unique "Witches' Market" where traditional remedies and offerings are sold.
- "Pisco Sour" is a popular cocktail made from pisco, a grape brandy produced in Chile and Peru.
- The "Lake of the Condors" in Peru is a high-altitude lake surrounded by impressive rock formations.
- The "Palacio Salvo" in Montevideo, Uruguay, was once the tallest building in South America and is known for its eclectic architecture.
- The "Yasuni National Park" in Ecuador is one of the most biodiverse places on Earth, with a single hectare containing more tree species than the entire United States.
- The "Paseo del Buen Pastor" in Argentina features a former women's prison converted into a cultural and artistic center.

- The "Church of San Francisco" in Lima, Peru, is renowned for its catacombs and unique library containing ancient texts.
- The "Uyuni Salt Flats" in Bolivia are so flat that they are used to calibrate satellite instruments.
- "Los Roques Archipelago" in Venezuela has crystal-clear waters and is a paradise for snorkelers and divers.
- "Chorizo" is a popular sausage dish enjoyed throughout South America.
- The "Yasuni ITT Initiative" in Ecuador aimed to protect a biodiverse region from oil drilling in exchange for international compensation.
- In "Chile," there is a town called "Punta Arenas," known for its strong winds and extreme temperatures.
- The "Teatro Colón" in Buenos Aires, Argentina, is one of the best opera houses in the world.
- "The Atahualpa Olympic Stadium" in Quito, Ecuador, is situated at 2,850 meters (9,350 feet) above sea level, making it one of the highest-altitude stadiums in the world.
- "Sopa paraguaya" is a traditional Paraguayan dish that is more like a dense cornbread than a soup.
- "Lima," the capital of Peru, is the second-largest desert city in the world after Cairo, Egypt.
- "Kuelap" in Peru is a massive pre-Inca fortress located high in the Andes.
- "Asado" is a popular style of barbecue in Argentina and Uruguay.
- The "Río de la Plata" is the widest river in the world, separating Argentina and Uruguay.
- "Palmito" is a delicious heart of palm vegetable often used in South American cuisine.
- The "Quilotoa" crater lake in Ecuador is strikingly colored and surrounded by scenic mountains.
- The "Mata Atlântica" (Atlantic Forest) in Brazil is one of the most endangered and biodiverse forests in the world.
- "Itaipu Dam" in Paraguay and Brazil is one of the largest hydroelectric power plants in the world.
- "Tiradentes" is a Brazilian city with well-preserved colonial architecture.
- The "Baños de Agua Santa" in Ecuador is known for its hot springs and adventure sports.

- The "Socotra Island" in Venezuela is home to unique flora and fauna, including the "Dragon's Blood Tree."
- "Chile" is the longest north-south stretch of land in the world, extending for about 4,300 kilometers.
- The "Cotopaxi" volcano in Ecuador is one of the world's highest active volcanoes and is known for its nearly symmetrical cone.
- "Manaus," Brazil, is located in the heart of the Amazon Rainforest and can only be reached by boat or plane.
- The "City of Valparaiso" in Chile is famous for its colorful houses and unique street art.
- "Guanabara Bay" in Rio de Janeiro, Brazil, is one of the largest natural harbors in the world.
- The "Páramo del Sol" in Colombia is the largest and highest páramo ecosystem on the planet.
- "Chile" has one of the driest deserts in the world, the "Atacama Desert," and one of the wettest places, "Valdivian Rainforest."
- The "Torres del Paine National Park" in Chile is known for its striking granite peaks, vast glaciers, and turquoise lakes.
- The "Llullaillaco Volcano" in Argentina is home to the highest archaeological site in the world, where three mummified Inca children were found.
- "Tiwanaku" in Bolivia is an ancient archaeological site with impressive monolithic architecture.
- "Montevideo," Uruguay, is one of the most LGBTQ+ friendly cities in South America.
- The "Aguas Calientes" in Peru is the gateway to Machu Picchu and is known for its natural hot springs.
- "Paraguay" is known as the "Heart of South America" because of its location.
- The "Caminito Street Museum" in Buenos Aires, Argentina, is an open-air museum with colorful houses and tango performances.
- The "Utria National Park" in Colombia is one of the few places in the world where humpback whales come to give birth.
- "Valdivia" in Chile is famous for its annual beer festival, the "Valdivian Week."
- The "Iguazu National Park" in Argentina and Brazil is home to a diverse array of wildlife, including jaguars and tapirs.
- "La Paz," Bolivia, is the highest capital city in the world, located at an altitude of about 3,650 meters (11,975 feet) above sea level.

- The "Amazon River" is so vast that it contains more water than the next eight largest rivers combined.
- "Punta del Este" in Uruguay is a popular resort destination known for its stunning beaches and vibrant nightlife.
- "Venezuela" has more than 2,000 bird species, making it a paradise for birdwatchers.
- "Cerro Aconcagua" in Argentina is the highest peak in the Southern and Western Hemispheres, standing at 6,960.8 meters (22,837 feet).
- The "Museum of Gold" in Bogotá, Colombia, houses the world's largest collection of pre-Columbian gold artifacts.
- The "Pampas" in Argentina is a vast grassland known for its cattle ranching and gaucho culture.
- "Cordillera Huayhuash" in Peru is a renowned trekking destination, offering breathtaking mountain scenery.
- The "Brazilian Carnival" is one of the largest and most extravagant festivals in the world, attracting millions of tourists each year.
- The "Falkland Islands" are a British Overseas Territory located off the coast of Argentina.
- "Ecuador" is the closest country to the sun when measured from the Earth's center due to its location on the equator.
- The "Che Guevara Mausoleum" in Santa Clara, Cuba, houses the remains of the revolutionary icon Ernesto "Che" Guevara.
- "Paso de Jama" is a high-altitude mountain pass connecting Argentina and Chile.
- "Cueva de las Manos" in Argentina features prehistoric cave paintings dating back over 9,000 years.
- The "Giant Anteater" is the largest anteater species and is found throughout South America.
- The "Salar de Atacama" in Chile is the world's third-largest salt flat and is home to flamingos and other unique wildlife.
- "The Mask of El Dorado" is an ancient gold mask found in Colombia, depicting the indigenous chief of the Muisca people.
- The "Caribbean Coast" of South America is known for its beautiful beaches and vibrant culture.
- "Easter Island" is home to the "Rapa Nui National Park," a UNESCO World Heritage Site protecting the island's unique cultural and archaeological heritage.

- "Rurrenabaque," Bolivia, is the gateway to the Bolivian Amazon rainforest and offers opportunities for wildlife encounters.
- The "Antofagasta" region in Chile is one of the best places in the world to stargaze due to its clear skies and low light pollution.
- "Kaieteur Falls" in Guyana is one of the tallest single-drop waterfalls globally, about five times higher than Niagara Falls.
- The "Los Glaciares National Park" in Argentina is home to the iconic "Perito Moreno Glacier."
- "South Georgia and the South Sandwich Islands" are British Overseas Territories located in the Southern Ocean.
- "El Ceibo" in Bolivia is one of the oldest trees in the world, estimated to be over 3,000 years old.
- The "Mount Roraima" in Venezuela, Brazil, and Guyana inspired Sir Arthur Conan Doyle's novel "The Lost World."
- "La Guajira Desert" in Colombia is a unique desert located on the northernmost tip of South America, bordering the Caribbean Sea.
- The "Valparaiso Ascensor" in Chile is a historic funicular railway system that provides transportation between the city's hilly neighborhoods.
- The "Machu Picchu" in Peru is one of the New Seven Wonders of the World and a UNESCO World Heritage Site.
- "The Guyana Shield" is one of the oldest geological formations on Earth, dating back over two billion years.
- The "Fernando de Noronha" archipelago in Brazil is a UNESCO World Heritage Site and is known for its pristine beaches and diverse marine life.
- The "Ojos del Salado" in Chile is the highest volcano on Earth, reaching an elevation of 6,893 meters (22,615 feet).
- "Guyana" has the highest percentage of rainforest cover in the world, with over 80% of its land covered in tropical forests.
- The "Infiernillo Gorge" in Bolivia is home to the "Devil's Tooth" rock formation, resembling a large, menacing canine.
- "Uruguay" is known for its progressive policies, including being the first country in the world to fully legalize marijuana.
- The "Cerro Tronador" in Argentina is a volcano known for the thunderous noise caused by falling ice from its glaciers.
- The "Marble Caves" in Chile are natural rock formations sculpted by the waters of Lake General Carrera.

- The "Giant River Otter" is the largest species of otter in the world and is found in the Amazon Rainforest.
- "Piranhas," known for their sharp teeth and fierce reputation, are native to the rivers of South America.
- The "Reserva Nacional Pacaya-Samiria" in Peru is the largest national reserve in the country, preserving vital Amazonian ecosystems.
- "Papaya" is a popular tropical fruit grown in many South American countries.
- The "Pululahua Geobotanical Reserve" in Ecuador is one of the few inhabited volcanic calderas in the world.
- "The Atacama Giant" in Chile is the largest prehistoric anthropomorphic geoglyph on Earth, carved into the side of a hill.
- "Paraguay" is one of the few landlocked countries in South America, bordered by Argentina, Brazil, and Bolivia.
- The "Arequipa Region" in Peru is known for its picturesque "Colca Canyon," one of the world's deepest canyons.
- "The Llaima Volcano" in Chile is one of the country's most active volcanoes and has erupted multiple times in recent history.
- The "Palm Groves of Elche" in Ecuador are UNESCO World Heritage-listed palm forests and the largest of their kind in the world.
- "The Pantanal" in Brazil is one of the best places in the world for wildlife viewing, particularly for spotting jaguars and anacondas.
- "Carnaval de Oruro" in Bolivia is a colorful festival celebrating Andean folklore, music, and dance.
- The "Amazon River" has over 2,200 known fish species, the highest diversity of any river on Earth.
- "The Church of St. George" in Ethiopia is famous for its underground monolithic rock-hewn churches, similar to those found in South America.
- The "Marajó Island" in Brazil is one of the world's largest freshwater islands and is home to a rich cultural heritage.
- "Easter Island" has around 900 moai statues, many of which remain unfinished at the quarry.
- The "Pisco Elqui" in Chile is known for producing the eponymous grape brandy, "pisco."

- The "Alerce Andino National Park" in Chile is home to some of the oldest living trees on Earth, "alerce" trees that can live for thousands of years.
- "Colombia" is the second-most biodiverse country in the world, after Brazil.
- "Ushuaia" in Argentina is often called the "End of the World" due to its southernmost location.
- The "Guajira Peninsula" in Colombia is home to the indigenous Wayuu people, known for their colorful handwoven bags and hammocks.
- "Chile" is one of the best places in the world for stargazing, with many observatories situated in the Atacama Desert.
- The "Ballestas Islands" in Peru are nicknamed the "Poor Man's Galápagos" and are home to a diverse range of wildlife.
- The "Andes Mountain Range" runs through seven South American countries, making it the longest mountain range in the world.
- "Cuyabeno Wildlife Reserve" in Ecuador is a remote and biodiverse area known for its unique flooded forest ecosystem.
- The "Jaguar" is the third-largest big cat in the world and is found in various South American countries.
- "Fitz Roy" in Argentina is a stunning mountain peak known for its challenging climbing routes.
- The "Hand of the Desert" is a famous sculpture located in the Atacama Desert of Chile.
- The "Potosí" in Bolivia is famous for its "Cerro Rico" (Rich Hill), which was once the world's largest silver mine.
- "Tierra del Fuego" is a region shared by Argentina and Chile, known for its rugged landscapes and unique wildlife.
- "Peru" is one of the world's largest producers of quinoa, a nutritious grain native to the Andes.
- "The Salt Cathedral of Zipaquirá" in Colombia is an underground church built inside a salt mine.
- "Iberá Wetlands" in Argentina is one of the largest wetland ecosystems in the world, home to various endangered species.
- "Tepuis" are unique table-top mountains found in Venezuela, Guyana, and Brazil.
- The "Macaw" is a vibrantly colored parrot species native to the rainforests of South America.
- "The Fitz Roy Massif" in Argentina is a striking mountain range known for its challenging rock climbing routes.

- The "Uros Floating Islands" in Peru are artificial islands made of reeds, inhabited by the Uru people.
- The "Camino de los Siete Lagos" (Seven Lakes Route) in Argentina is a scenic road that passes through seven beautiful mountain lakes.
- The "Bicentennial Tower" in Buenos Aires, Argentina, is the tallest tower in South America, standing at 220 meters (722 feet) tall.
- "Manaus," Brazil, is known as the "Heart of the Amazon" and serves as a major gateway to the rainforest.
- The "Península Valdés" in Argentina is a UNESCO World Heritage Site and a crucial breeding ground for Southern Right Whales.
- "Chachapoyas" in Peru is known as the "City of Clouds" due to its frequent foggy weather.
- The "Amazon Rainforest" is estimated to contain over 400 billion individual trees, representing approximately 16,000 species.
- "Tepui" mountains are believed to have inspired Sir Arthur Conan Doyle's novel "The Lost World."
- "Iguazu Falls" is taller than Niagara Falls and twice as wide, making it one of the most awe-inspiring waterfalls on Earth.
- "The Magdalena River" in Colombia is the longest river in the country, running for about 1,528 kilometers (949 miles).
- The "Andean Condor" is the largest flying bird in the world and is found in the Andes mountain range.
- "Barranquilla" in Colombia hosts one of the largest carnival celebrations in the world, second only to Rio de Janeiro's carnival.
- The "Potosí Mint" in Bolivia was once the main mint of the Spanish Empire, producing vast amounts of silver coins.
- The "Carnaval de Negros y Blancos" in Colombia celebrates diversity and cultural heritage through a unique and vibrant parade.
- The "Interoceanic Highway" connects the Atlantic and Pacific Oceans, passing through Brazil, Peru, and Bolivia.
- "Samaipata" in Bolivia is home to a mysterious archaeological site known as "El Fuerte," featuring intricate carvings in the rock.
- The "Cerro de la Silla" in Mexico is a famous hill with a saddle-like shape, making it a recognizable landmark.

- The "Santos Dumont" in Brazil was one of the first cities in the world to have an organized air traffic control system.
- "The Galápagos Tortoise" is the largest species of tortoise and can live for over 100 years.
- "Yungas Road" in Bolivia is notoriously known as "Death Road" due to its treacherous conditions and high number of accidents.
- The "Guyana Space Center" in French Guiana is a major launch site for European and international space missions.
- "The Loro Tricahue National Reserve" in Chile protects the critically endangered "Tricahue Parrot" species.
- "The Salt Flats of Maras" in Peru have been in use since pre-Inca times for salt extraction.
- "Bogotá," Colombia's capital, is located at an altitude of approximately 2,640 meters (8,660 feet) above sea level.
- The "Oro del Rhin" in Bolivia is a historic and iconic neo-Gothic building, now functioning as a cultural center.
- "The Uchumayo Geoglyphs" in Peru are ancient geometric figures etched into the earth.
- "La Candelaria" in Bogotá, Colombia, is the city's historic center, known for its colonial architecture and vibrant street art.
- "The Piedra del Peñol" in Colombia is a massive granite rock with a staircase leading to its summit, offering panoramic views of the surrounding landscape.
- "Kuélap" in Peru is a pre-Inca archaeological site located on a mountaintop, resembling a fortress.
- The "Mburucuyá National Park" in Argentina is a hotspot for birdwatching, with over 350 bird species documented.
- "El León Dormido" (The Sleeping Lion) is a rock formation off the coast of Ecuador, resembling a resting lion.
- "Salta," Argentina, is known for its well-preserved colonial architecture and historical sites.
- The "São Paulo Museum of Art" in Brazil is one of the most important art museums in Latin America.
- "The Strokkur Geyser" in Chile is a powerful geyser known for its frequent eruptions.
- The "Tren a las Nubes" (Train to the Clouds) in Argentina is one of the highest train routes in the world, reaching an altitude of 4,220 meters (13,845 feet).
- "Río Cañete" in Peru is famous for its unique annual "Dança de los Diablos" (Dance of the Devils) festival.

- The "Volcanoes Avenue" in Ecuador is a scenic route that passes by numerous volcanoes, including the "Cotopaxi."
- "The Mercado Central" in Santiago, Chile, is a bustling market known for its fresh produce and traditional food stalls.
- "Corcovado National Park" in Costa Rica is one of the most biodiverse places on Earth, with 2.5% of the world's biodiversity in a small area.
- "Chicamocha Canyon" in Colombia is one of the largest canyons in the world, deeper than the Grand Canyon in some parts.
- "The Islas Ballestas" in Peru are home to hundreds of thousands of seabirds, sea lions, and penguins.
- The "Aconcagua Provincial Park" in Argentina is home to the highest peak in the Southern Hemisphere, "Cerro Aconcagua."
- "Montevideo," Uruguay's capital, is known for its beautiful beaches and vibrant cultural scene.
- The "Stone Tree" in Bolivia's "Eduardo Avaroa Andean Fauna National Reserve" is a natural rock formation resembling a tree.
- The "Paracas Candelabra" in Peru is a massive geoglyph etched into the desert, similar to the Nazca Lines.
- "The Church of San Francisco" in Quito, Ecuador, is adorned with intricate golden decorations, earning it the nickname "The Golden Church."
- "Lake Titicaca" is the highest navigable lake in the world, situated between Peru and Bolivia.
- "Chapada Diamantina National Park" in Brazil is known for its stunning landscapes, waterfalls, and underground rivers.
- "Iguazu Falls" has a legend that says a deity planned to marry a woman, and in her escape, she turned into a waterfall, forming the falls.
- The "Church of San Pedro" in Copacabana, Bolivia, houses the "Virgen de Copacabana," a revered religious icon.
- "Punta Tombo" in Argentina is the largest Magellanic penguin colony in South America.
- The "Stone Forest" in Bolivia's "Eduardo Avaroa Andean Fauna National Reserve" consists of towering limestone columns.
- "Machu Picchu" is believed to have been a royal estate for the Inca emperor Pachacuti.
- The "Church of San Francisco" in Lima, Peru, contains catacombs that were once used as a burial site.

- "Bogotá," Colombia, has a unique public transportation system called the "TransMilenio," known for its dedicated bus lanes.
- The "Carnival of Barranquilla" in Colombia is a UNESCO Masterpiece of the Oral and Intangible Heritage of Humanity.
- "Cabo Polonio" in Uruguay is a remote and eco-friendly village with no electricity or running water.
- "The Moon Valley" in Chile's "Atacama Desert" has landscapes that resemble the surface of the moon.
- "Cueva de los Tayos" in Ecuador is a mysterious cave system with legends of hidden treasures and ancient artifacts.
- The "Torres del Paine" in Chile is home to unique geological formations, including the iconic "Las Torres."
- "Cristo del Pacífico" in Lima, Peru, is a large statue of Christ, resembling Rio de Janeiro's "Christ the Redeemer."
- The "Marble Cathedral" in Chile is a network of stunning marble caves on General Carrera Lake.
- "Mendoza" in Argentina is famous for its wine production, particularly Malbec.
- The "Golden Museum" in Colombia showcases an extensive collection of pre-Columbian gold artifacts.
- "Huacachina" in Peru is an oasis surrounded by sand dunes, offering thrilling sandboarding experiences.
- "Las Lajas Sanctuary" in Colombia is a neo-Gothic basilica built on a bridge over a gorge.
- "The Atacama Giant" in Chile is a massive geoglyph, representing a deity or an astronomical calendar.
- The "Beagle Channel" in Argentina is named after Charles Darwin's ship, HMS Beagle, which explored the region.
- "The Cathedral of Brasília" in Brazil is an architectural masterpiece designed by Oscar Niemeyer.
- "Mount Roraima" inspired the setting of Sir Arthur Conan Doyle's novel "The Lost World."
- The "Guayas River" in Ecuador is navigable for about 360 kilometers (224 miles) from the Gulf of Guayaquil.
- The "Peruvian Hairless Dog" is an ancient breed of dog native to Peru.
- "The Church of San Francisco" in La Paz, Bolivia, features a striking facade made of pink and grey stone.
- "Vilcabamba" in Ecuador is known as the "Valley of Longevity" due to the longevity of its inhabitants.

- "Lençóis Maranhenses National Park" in Brazil is famous for its vast sand dunes and seasonal lagoons.
- The "Machu Picchu Sanctuary Lodge" in Peru is the only hotel located within the archaeological site of Machu Picchu.
- The "San Rafael Glacier" in Chile is a massive glacier that calves into the San Rafael Lagoon.
- "The Battle of Ayacucho" in Peru was the final battle of the South American wars of independence.
- "Iquitos" in Peru is the world's largest city that is not connected to the global road network.
- The "Mapuche" people in Chile and Argentina have a rich cultural heritage and traditional ceremonies.
- "Tiahuanaco" in Bolivia is an ancient archaeological site and a UNESCO World Heritage Site.
- "Cabo de la Vela" in Colombia is a remote desert region with stunning beaches and turquoise waters.
- "The Great Inca Trail" is a network of roads connecting important Inca sites across Peru and other Andean countries.
- The "Ouro Preto" in Brazil is a UNESCO World Heritage Site known for its well-preserved colonial architecture.
- "Mount Chimborazo" in Ecuador is the farthest point from the center of the Earth due to the planet's oblate shape.
- "Tiradentes" in Brazil is a charming colonial town known for its cobblestone streets and historic buildings.
- The "Teatro Colón" in Buenos Aires, Argentina, is one of the world's most renowned opera houses.
- "The Church of Las Lajas" in Colombia is built into the side of a canyon and is a pilgrimage site for Catholics.
- The "Altiplano" is a high plateau stretching across several South American countries, known for its stunning landscapes.
- "The Palace of the Governors" in Bolivia is one of the oldest colonial buildings in South America.
- "The Palm Jumeirah" in Dubai was inspired by the shape of the "Isla Margarita" in Venezuela.
- The "Chacaltaya Ski Resort" in Bolivia was the world's highest ski resort before its glacier melted.
- "The Basilica of Our Lady of Copacabana" in Bolivia is a prominent pilgrimage site for Catholics.
- "The Perito Moreno Glacier" in Argentina is one of the few advancing glaciers in the world.

- "Petrobras" in Brazil is one of the largest oil companies in the world.
- "Quilotoa" in Ecuador is a stunning volcanic crater lake with vivid turquoise waters.
- "Cueva del Milodón" in Chile is known for its large cave and the discovery of a prehistoric giant ground sloth.
- "El Tatio Geysers" in Chile is one of the highest geyser fields globally, with eruptions at sunrise.
- "The Pampas" in Argentina is a vast grassland region famous for its gauchos and cattle ranches.
- "Caño Cristales" in Colombia is known as the "River of Five Colors" due to its vibrant hues.
- "Cueva de las Manos" in Argentina contains ancient cave paintings dating back over 9,000 years.
- "La Paz" in Bolivia is the highest capital city in the world, sitting at an altitude of around 3,650 meters (11,975 feet).
- "Llanos" in Colombia and Venezuela is a vast tropical grassland known for its wildlife diversity.
- "Paraná River" in South America is the second-longest river on the continent, after the Amazon.
- "Boca Juniors" and "River Plate" are two of the most famous football clubs in Argentina, known for their intense rivalry.
- "The Central University of Venezuela" in Caracas is considered a masterpiece of modern architecture.
- "El Pailón del Diablo" in Ecuador is a magnificent waterfall known as the "Devil's Cauldron."
- "Isla de los Estados" in Argentina is one of the most remote islands in the world, known for its rugged landscapes.
- "Cali" in Colombia is famous for its salsa music and dance culture.
- "The Jirón Street" in Peru is one of the oldest streets in Lima, lined with historic buildings.
- "Lençóis Maranhenses National Park" in Brazil has a unique landscape of white sand dunes and turquoise lagoons.
- "Colca Canyon" in Peru is one of the world's deepest canyons, nearly twice as deep as the Grand Canyon.
- "Maracanã Stadium" in Brazil is one of the largest football stadiums globally and hosted two FIFA World Cup finals.
- "The Galapagos Shark" is a species of shark found in the Galápagos Islands.

- "Lake Poopó" in Bolivia is a saline lake that experienced significant drying due to climate change.
- "Cerros de Mavecure" in Colombia are impressive rock formations rising from the jungle floor.
- "Itaipu Dam" on the Paraná River is one of the largest hydroelectric power plants in the world.
- "The Way of the Cross" in Brazil is the largest outdoor amphitheater for passion plays.
- "Kaieteur Falls" in Guyana is one of the most powerful single-drop waterfalls in the world.
- "Villa de Leyva" in Colombia is a well-preserved colonial town with cobblestone streets.
- "Lagoa do Fogo" in Azores, Portugal, shares its name with a lagoon in the Azores.
- "Huaca Pucllana" in Peru is an archaeological site featuring an adobe and clay pyramid.
- "São João Batista" in Brazil is a UNESCO World Heritage Site known for its colonial architecture.
- "Mount Roraima" inspired the setting of the movie "Up" by Disney Pixar.
- "The Easter Island Script" is an undeciphered script found on Easter Island.
- "Parque Nacional Los Glaciares" in Argentina is home to numerous glaciers, including the famous Perito Moreno Glacier.
- "The Devil's Nose Train" in Ecuador is a thrilling train journey down a steep mountain slope.
- "The Andean Flamingo" is a unique species of flamingo found in the Andes mountain range.
- "The Pantanal" in Brazil is the world's largest tropical wetland, known for its incredible biodiversity.
- "Eje Cafetero" in Colombia is known for its coffee production and picturesque coffee plantations.
- "Cueva del Indio" in Puerto Rico is an archaeological site with petroglyphs created by the Taíno people.
- "The Capuchin Monkey" is a small monkey species found in the rainforests of South America.
- "The Torres del Paine" in Chile are a set of three distinct granite peaks in the national park of the same name.
- The "Easter Island Horse" is a unique breed of small horse found on Easter Island.

- "Cotopaxi National Park" in Ecuador is home to the Cotopaxi volcano, one of the highest active volcanoes in the world.
- "The San Rafael Glacier" in Chile is a massive glacier that calves icebergs into the San Rafael Lagoon.
- The "Sambadrome" in Rio de Janeiro, Brazil, is a stadium where the famous Carnival parade takes place.
- "The Andean Cat" is a small, elusive wildcat found in the high Andes mountains.

Chapter 6: Australia

- Australia is the world's sixth-largest country by land area.
- Australia is the only country in the world that covers an entire continent.
- The Great Barrier Reef off the coast of Queensland is the largest coral reef system in the world.
- Canberra, not Sydney or Melbourne, is the capital city of Australia.
- The kangaroo and emu are featured on Australia's coat of arms because they are animals that cannot move backward, symbolizing progress.
- Australia has the highest population of wild camels in the world.
- The world's largest sand island, Fraser Island, is located off the coast of Queensland, Australia.
- The Sydney Opera House is one of the most famous and iconic buildings in the world.

- Australia has over 10,000 beaches, which would take over 27 years to visit if you visited one every day.
- The Great Victoria Desert is the largest desert in Australia and the second-largest in the world.
- The Box Jellyfish found in Australian waters is one of the deadliest creatures on Earth.
- The Australian Alps receive more snowfall than the Swiss Alps.
- The Dingo is a wild dog native to Australia and is one of the continent's most ancient animals.
- The largest monolith in the world, Uluru (Ayers Rock), is located in the heart of Australia.
- Melbourne, Australia, has been consistently ranked as one of the most livable cities in the world.
- Australia is home to the longest fence in the world, the "Dingo Fence," built to protect livestock from wild dogs.
- The Tasmanian Devil is a carnivorous marsupial found only in Tasmania, Australia.
- The Nullarbor Plain in Australia is the world's largest limestone karst landscape.
- Australia is the world's largest exporter of wool.
- New Zealand is home to the world's only alpine parrot, the Kea.
- Australia's national gemstone is the opal, found in abundance in the country.
- The Pacific Ocean is the largest and deepest ocean in the world, covering one-third of the Earth's surface.
- New Zealand has no native land mammals, except for bats.
- The Australian Capital Territory (ACT) has a "Bush Capital" design, with half of its area reserved for nature parks and forests.
- The highest mountain in Australia is Mount Kosciuszko.
- New Zealand was the first country to grant women the right to vote in 1893.
- The "Dugong" or "sea cow" is a marine mammal found in the waters of northern Australia and nearby islands.
- Oceania is home to the world's smallest independent country, Nauru.
- The famous New Zealand film series "The Lord of the Rings" and "The Hobbit" were filmed entirely in New Zealand.
- The "Māori" are the indigenous people of New Zealand, known for their rich cultural heritage.

- The currency of Australia is the Australian Dollar, and New Zealand uses the New Zealand Dollar.
- The indigenous people of Australia are known as Aboriginal and Torres Strait Islander peoples.
- New Zealand is located on two tectonic plates, making it a hotspot for geothermal activity.
- The Kookaburra, a bird native to Australia, is known for its distinctive laughing call.
- Oceania is home to the largest living lizard, the Komodo dragon, found in Indonesia.
- The "Didgeridoo" is a traditional wind instrument created by Aboriginal people in Australia.
- The indigenous people of New Zealand, the Māori, have a traditional war dance called the "Haka."
- New Zealand has more sheep than people, with over 29 million sheep.
- The Great Dividing Range in Australia is the third-longest mountain range in the world.
- Oceania is home to the world's largest saltwater crocodile species, the Saltwater Crocodile.
- Australia's "Wave Rock" in Western Australia is a natural rock formation shaped like a giant ocean wave.
- New Zealand's "Waitomo Glowworm Caves" are famous for their luminescent glowworms.
- The Kakadu National Park in Australia is a UNESCO World Heritage site and one of the world's great wilderness areas.
- Oceania has the world's smallest country by land area, Vatican City, located within Rome, Italy.
- The Kiwi, a flightless bird, is the national symbol of New Zealand.
- The Gold Coast in Queensland, Australia, is famous for its theme parks and golden beaches.
- Oceania's largest city by population is Sydney, Australia.
- New Zealand's national rugby team, the "All Blacks," is one of the most successful rugby teams in the world.
- The Great Ocean Road in Australia is known for its stunning coastal views and rock formations like the Twelve Apostles.
- Oceania is home to the unique "Tuatara," a reptile with ancient origins that predates dinosaurs.
- The "Platypus" is a unique Australian mammal known for laying eggs and having a duck-like bill.

- Oceania's largest city by land area is Brisbane, Australia.
- New Zealand is home to the world's smallest dolphin species, the Hector's dolphin.
- Australia's "Pinnacles Desert" in Western Australia features thousands of limestone pillars rising from the sand.
- The island of Niue in Oceania is known for its stunning limestone caves and unique sea tracks.
- The Great Barrier Reef Marine Park in Australia is larger than the United Kingdom and Switzerland combined.
- Oceania is home to the world's largest ocean, the Pacific Ocean.
- The Mauna Kea volcano in Hawaii, Oceania, is the world's tallest mountain when measured from its base on the ocean floor.
- Australia's "Wave Rock" in Western Australia is a natural rock formation shaped like a giant ocean wave.
- The "Kiwifruit" originated in China but was named after New Zealand's national symbol, the Kiwi.
- The famous Lord of the Rings film trilogy was directed by New Zealander Peter Jackson.
- Australia has over 60 designated wine regions, known for producing some of the world's finest wines.
- The Oceania region is home to many unique marine species, including the Mola Mola, the world's heaviest bony fish.
- New Zealand's "Rotorua" is known for its geothermal activity, with bubbling mud pools and colorful hot springs.
- Australia is home to the world's longest fence, the "Dingo Fence," stretching over 5,600 kilometers.
- The Māori people of New Zealand have a traditional method of cooking using heated rocks buried in a pit called the "Hangi."
- The Torres Strait Islands between Australia and Papua New Guinea are known for their rich indigenous culture.
- The blue and white colors of New Zealand's flag represent the Southern Cross constellation and the country's maritime heritage.
- Australia is home to the world's largest population of wild camels.
- The "Kiwi" fruit was originally known as the "Chinese gooseberry" before being named after the Kiwi bird.
- The Cook Islands in Oceania is named after Captain James Cook, the British explorer.

- Australia's "Fraser Island" is the only place in the world where rainforest grows on sand.
- The "Tā Moko" is the traditional Māori facial tattoo art, each design is unique and carries cultural significance.
- New Zealand has the world's steepest street, "Baldwin Street" in Dunedin.
- Australia has over 50 million kangaroos, which outnumber the human population.
- The island of Bora Bora in French Polynesia is famous for its turquoise lagoon and overwater bungalows.
- The Sydney Harbour Bridge and the Opera House were both designed by Danish architect Jørn Utzon.
- The "Abel Tasman National Park" in New Zealand was named after the Dutch explorer Abel Tasman.
- The Oceania region has the world's largest collection of coral reefs.
- Australia's "Kangaroo Island" is home to the world's only pure-bred population of Ligurian bees.
- The Tuvalu Atolls in Oceania are some of the lowest-lying islands on Earth.
- New Zealand has no native snakes.
- Australia is home to the world's largest population of wild dingoes.
- The Pitcairn Islands, a British Overseas Territory, is one of the least populous territories in the world.
- Oceania has some of the world's rarest bird species, including the Kakapo and the Black-winged Petrel.
- Australia's "Lake Hillier" in Western Australia is famously pink due to its high salt content.
- The Solomon Islands in Oceania are known for their diverse indigenous cultures and languages.
- New Zealand has more species of penguins than any other country.
- The "Yarralumla Nursery" in Australia is the world's largest supplier of plants for international embassies.
- Oceania is home to the world's largest known tree, the "Hyperion" redwood tree in California.
- Australia's "Kangaroo Island" is known for its abundance of kangaroos, koalas, and sea lions.
- The Great Barrier Reef is so vast that it can be seen from space.
- The "Koala" is not a bear but a marsupial native to Australia.

- New Zealand has more sheep than people, with a ratio of about seven sheep for every person.
- The Oceania region is known for its diverse range of indigenous art, including bark paintings, wood carvings, and tapa cloth.
- The Aboriginal people of Australia have a rich tradition of rock art, some of which dates back tens of thousands of years.
- The "Cook Islands" are a self-governing country in free association with New Zealand.
- Australia's "Bungle Bungle Range" in Western Australia is famous for its unique beehive-shaped rock formations.
- The "Niuean Flying Fox" is a unique bat species found on the island of Niue.
- The "Australian Alps" receive more snowfall than Switzerland.
- Oceania's "Papua New Guinea" is home to over 800 indigenous languages, making it one of the most linguistically diverse places in the world.
- The indigenous people of Hawaii, known as "Kanaka Maoli," have a deep cultural connection to the land and sea.
- Australia's "Shark Bay" is home to the largest seagrass meadow in the world, covering an area of over 4,800 square kilometers.
- The "Mangrove Finch" is a critically endangered bird species found only in the Galapagos Islands, an overseas territory of Ecuador in Oceania.
- The "Whale Shark" found in Oceania's waters is the largest fish species in the world.
- The Great Ocean Road in Australia is known for its "Twelve Apostles," a series of limestone stacks standing in the ocean.
- New Zealand has one of the world's highest bungee jumps, the "Nevis Bungy," with a drop of over 134 meters.
- Australia's "Sydney Harbour Bridge" is affectionately nicknamed "The Coathanger."
- The Solomon Islands are renowned for their exquisite handcrafted shell money, known as "Tabu."
- New Zealand's "Rotorua" is known for its geothermal activity, with bubbling mud pools and colorful hot springs.
- Australia's "Cockatoo Island" in Sydney Harbour has served as a convict prison, industrial school, and shipyard.
- The Tuvalu Atolls in Oceania are some of the lowest-lying islands on Earth.
- New Zealand is home to the world's oldest tree, a Kauri tree called "Tāne Mahuta."

- The Norfolk Island Pine, a symbol of the island of Norfolk Island, is not native to the island but is instead native to New Caledonia.
- Australia's "Gippsland Lakes" is the largest navigable inland waterway in Australia.
- The "Hawaiian Monk Seal" is one of the rarest seal species and is native to Hawaii.
- The traditional dance form of the "Haka" is performed not only by the Māori of New Zealand but also by the national rugby team, the "All Blacks," before matches.
- Oceania is home to the world's largest fish, the "Whale Shark," and the world's smallest fish, the "Paedocypris progenetica" found in Indonesia.
- The "Gold Coast" in Queensland, Australia, is famous for its theme parks and golden beaches.
- New Zealand's "Milford Sound" is often called the "Eighth Wonder of the World" for its breathtaking natural beauty.
- Australia is home to the world's largest population of wild dingoes.
- Oceania's "Great Barrier Reef" is home to around 1,500 species of fish and more than 400 types of coral.
- Australia's "Wave Rock" in Western Australia is a natural rock formation shaped like a giant ocean wave.
- The "Kiwifruit" originated in China but was named after New Zealand's national symbol, the Kiwi.
- The famous Lord of the Rings film trilogy was directed by New Zealander Peter Jackson.
- Australia has over 60 designated wine regions, known for producing some of the world's finest wines.
- The Oceania region is home to many unique marine species, including the Mola Mola, the world's heaviest bony fish.
- The "New Caledonian Crow" is known for its exceptional problem-solving abilities, using tools to obtain food.
- Oceania's "Polynesian Triangle" encompasses the Hawaiian Islands, New Zealand, and Easter Island.
- The "Coconut Crab" found on some Pacific islands is the world's largest terrestrial crab.
- Australia's "Karijini National Park" in Western Australia is famous for its deep gorges and stunning rock formations.
- The "Pitcairn Islands" are the last British overseas territory in the Pacific Ocean.

- The Great Barrier Reef is home to the "Dwarf Minke Whale," which is known for its curious and interactive behavior with snorkelers and divers.
- The "Kiwi" bird has a keen sense of smell, which is unusual for a bird, and uses it to find food underground.
- Australia's "Whitehaven Beach" in Queensland is known for its pristine white silica sand and crystal-clear waters.
- The Galapagos Islands, an overseas territory of Ecuador in Oceania, inspired Charles Darwin's theory of evolution by natural selection.
- New Zealand's "Aoraki/Mount Cook" is the country's highest peak, and its name means "Cloud Piercer."
- Oceania is home to the world's most isolated population center, the "Pitcairn Islands."
- Australia's "Cable Beach" in Western Australia is famous for its camel rides along the coast at sunset.
- The "Green Sea Turtle" found in Oceania's waters is known for its migration across vast distances.
- Australia's "Great Victoria Desert" is the world's largest sand dune desert.
- Oceania's "Easter Island" is home to the iconic "Moai" statues, which were carved by the Rapa Nui people.
- New Zealand has the world's steepest street, "Baldwin Street," with a gradient of 35%.
- The "Moa" was a large flightless bird that once lived in New Zealand and went extinct around 500 years ago.
- Oceania's "Christmas Island" is famous for the mass migration of millions of red crabs to the sea.
- Australia's "Kangaroo Island" is known for its abundant wildlife, including kangaroos, koalas, and sea lions.
- The "Kilauea" volcano in Hawaii, Oceania, is one of the world's most active volcanoes.
- The "Papua New Guinean Singing Dog" is a rare and ancient breed of dog native to Papua New Guinea.
- New Zealand's "Waitomo Glowworm Caves" are famous for their luminescent glowworms.
- The "Tasman Sea" separates Australia from New Zealand.
- Australia's "Great Ocean Road" is one of the world's most scenic coastal drives, spanning 243 kilometers.
- The "Manta Ray" found in Oceania's waters is one of the largest rays in the world, with wingspans reaching up to 7 meters.

- The "Norfolk Island Pine," native to New Caledonia, is grown as a popular Christmas tree in many countries.
- New Zealand's "Waitomo Glowworm Caves" are famous for their luminescent glowworms.
- The "Galapagos Tortoise" found in the Galapagos Islands is the largest tortoise species in the world.
- Oceania is home to some of the world's most active volcanoes, including "Mount Yasur" in Vanuatu.
- Australia's "Shark Bay" is home to the world's largest population of dugongs, also known as sea cows.
- The "Papua New Guinean Huli Wigmen" are known for their intricate and elaborate wigs made from their own hair.
- New Zealand's "Milford Sound" is known for its breathtaking waterfalls, including the "Stirling Falls," one of the tallest in the country.
- The "Didgeridoo" is a traditional wind instrument created by Aboriginal people in Australia.
- Australia's "Whitsunday Islands" are named after the day they were discovered by Captain Cook - the Christian festival of Whitsun or Pentecost.
- The indigenous people of New Caledonia, known as "Kanak," have a rich cultural heritage that includes intricate sculptures and traditional dances.
- The Solomon Islands in Oceania are known for their "Shell Money," a traditional form of currency made from shell discs.
- Oceania's "Fiji" is famous for its clear blue waters and vibrant coral reefs, making it a popular destination for snorkelers and divers.
- The "Hawaiian Green Sea Turtle," known as "Honu," is a symbol of good luck and longevity in Hawaiian culture.
- Australia's "Lord Howe Island" is a UNESCO World Heritage site and is home to several unique species found nowhere else on Earth.
- The "Hawaiian Islands" were formed by volcanic activity, with the youngest island, "Hawaii," still growing due to ongoing eruptions.
- New Zealand's "Kaikoura" is renowned for its excellent whale-watching opportunities, including encounters with sperm whales.
- Oceania's "Tahiti" is the largest island in French Polynesia and is often associated with the concept of a tropical paradise.

- The indigenous people of New Guinea, known as "Papua," have over 1,000 distinct languages spoken among their various tribes.
- The "Abel Tasman National Park" in New Zealand was named after the Dutch explorer Abel Tasman.
- Australia's "Kakadu National Park" is not only famous for its natural beauty but also for its rich Aboriginal rock art, some of which is over 20,000 years old.
- Oceania is home to the "Melanesian Choirs," renowned for their beautiful harmonies and performances during cultural events.
- The "Daintree Rainforest" in Australia is one of the oldest rainforests in the world, dating back over 135 million years.
- New Zealand's "Fox and Franz Josef Glaciers" are unique as they descend to just 300 meters above sea level in a temperate rainforest.
- Oceania's "Niue" is known as the "Rock of Polynesia" due to its coral formations and limestone cliffs.
- Australia's "Uluru-Kata Tjuta National Park" is not only home to the iconic Uluru but also to the stunning rock formations known as Kata Tjuta (the Olgas).
- The "Mangrove Finch" is one of the rarest birds in the world, found only in the Galapagos Islands.
- The "Southern Cross" constellation, a symbol of the southern hemisphere, can be seen from various countries in Oceania.
- Australia's "The Pinnacles" in Nambung National Park feature thousands of limestone pillars, creating an otherworldly landscape.
- Oceania's "New Guinea" is the second-largest island in the world, after Greenland.
- The "Teahupo'o" wave in Tahiti, French Polynesia, is known as one of the world's heaviest and most dangerous waves for surfers.
- Australia's "Royal Flying Doctor Service" provides medical aid to people living in remote areas and is one of the largest and most comprehensive aeromedical organizations globally.
- The "Marquesas Islands" in French Polynesia are believed to be the most isolated archipelago in the world.
- Oceania's "New Caledonia" is one of the world's largest producers of nickel.
- The "Daintree Rainforest" in Australia is home to the endangered "Cassowary," a large and colorful flightless bird.

- New Zealand's "Aoraki/Mount Cook" is a popular destination for mountaineers and climbers.
- Oceania's "Bora Bora" is a famous luxury travel destination, known for its overwater bungalows and turquoise lagoon.
- Australia's "Tasmanian Devil" is the largest carnivorous marsupial in the world and is endemic to Tasmania.
- The "Na Pali Coast" in Hawaii, Oceania, is famous for its rugged cliffs and lush green valleys.
- The "Great Barrier Reef" is home to one of the world's largest colonies of "Nemo" - the popular clownfish.
- New Zealand's "Fiordland National Park" is known for its spectacular fjords and waterfalls.
- Oceania's "Vanuatu" is an archipelago of over 80 islands known for its unique blend of traditional Melanesian culture and outdoor adventures.
- Australia's "Ningaloo Reef" is famous for its annual whale shark migration, where visitors can swim with these gentle giants.
- The "Tuamotu Archipelago" in French Polynesia is composed of more than 70 coral atolls.
- Oceania's "Coral Triangle" is known as the "Amazon of the Seas" due to its incredible marine biodiversity.
- The "Gold Coast" in Queensland, Australia, is home to the Southern Hemisphere's biggest theme park, "Dreamworld."
- The "Galapagos Islands" are home to unique species such as the "Galapagos Tortoise" and the "Blue-footed Booby."
- Oceania's "Nauru" is the third-smallest country in the world by land area.
- Australia's "Kings Canyon" in the Northern Territory is famous for its breathtaking sandstone cliffs and ancient rock formations.
- The "Volcanic Islands" in Tonga are known for their stunning volcanic landscapes and friendly locals.
- Oceania's "Mokohinau Islands" in New Zealand are a haven for seabirds and marine life, including fur seals and dolphins.
- The "Great White Shark" is found in the waters of Australia, and "Shark Cage Diving" is a popular activity for thrill-seekers.
- New Zealand's "Whangarei Falls" is a beautiful waterfall surrounded by lush greenery.
- Oceania's "Samoa" is known for its vibrant traditional dance called the "Siva Samoa."

- The "Tui" bird in New Zealand is known for its unique and melodic song, which can imitate various sounds, including human speech.
- Australia's "Coober Pedy" is an underground town where most of the residents live in homes dug into the earth to escape the extreme heat.
- The island of "Tanna" in Vanuatu is home to the "John Frum" cult, which believes in the return of an American messiah who will bring wealth and prosperity.
- The "Norfolk Island" once had its own language known as "Norf'k," which is a mix of English and Tahitian.
- Australia's "Lake McKenzie" on Fraser Island is so pure and clean that it is believed to have healing properties for the skin.
- The "Kohola Brewery" in Hawaii creates beer using deep ocean water, making it the world's first brewery to do so.
- The "Bone Church" in New Zealand is an eerie church adorned with human bones, primarily from deceased Māori.
- The "Kiribati" islands are at risk of becoming uninhabitable due to rising sea levels caused by climate change.
- Australia's "Cockatoo Island" was once a prison and later a shipyard, making it one of the country's most historically significant sites.
- The tiny "Nauru" is known for having the world's highest rate of obesity, mainly due to a diet heavy in imported processed foods.
- The "Hobbiton" movie set in New Zealand, used in "The Lord of the Rings" and "The Hobbit" film trilogies, is a popular tourist attraction.
- The "Papua New Guinea" is home to one of the world's largest butterflies, the "Queen Alexandra's Birdwing."
- The "Whale Rider" is a famous New Zealand film about a young Māori girl who defies tradition to become a leader.
- The "Ogasawara" islands in Japan, also known as the "Galapagos of the Orient," are home to unique and endemic species.
- "Mount Wilhelm" in Papua New Guinea is the highest mountain in Oceania outside of New Guinea and Australia.
- Australia's "Kangaroo Island" was almost named "Kangarooa," but a spelling mistake on a British map resulted in the current name.
- The "Cook Islands" have their own currency, the "Cook Islands dollar," which is separate from the New Zealand dollar.

- The "Tasmanian Tiger" or thylacine was native to Tasmania and is believed to be extinct since the 1930s.
- "Daintree Rainforest" is the only place where two World Heritage-listed sites meet – the rainforest and the Great Barrier Reef.
- The "Galapagos Tortoise" can live for over 100 years, and some individuals may reach more than 200 years.
- The world's largest known egg, from a now-extinct bird called the "Elephant Bird," was discovered in Madagascar.
- The island of "Pohnpei" in Micronesia is home to the ancient city of "Nan Madol," built on a series of artificial islets.
- In New Zealand, it is illegal to name a child anything that resembles an official title, such as "King" or "Queen."
- The "Flying Fox" bat in Australia is not a fox at all, but a large fruit bat with a fox-like face.
- Oceania's "Christmas Island" is home to an annual red crab migration, where millions of crabs move to the sea to breed.
- The "Samoa" is known for "Fa'afafine," a traditional third gender recognized and accepted in the culture.
- Australia's "Kata Tjuta" rock formations are believed to be 500 million years older than "Uluru."
- The indigenous people of "Vanuatu" believe that their ancestors came from a mythical place called "Pentecost."
- The "Samoan Fire Knife Dance" involves dancers twirling a knife lit on fire, showcasing their agility and bravery.
- The "Australian White Ibis" is affectionately known as the "bin chicken" due to its scavenging habits in urban areas.
- "Yarralumla," a suburb in Australia's capital city Canberra, was once a temporary summer camp for Aboriginal people.
- The "Futuna" and "Wallis" islands are located in Oceania but are divided between two different countries, Vanuatu and France.
- The "Aboriginal Dreamtime" is a term used to describe the beliefs and stories of Australia's indigenous people about the creation of the world.
- The "Gold Coast" in Australia got its name not from gold mines but from the 1950s real estate promotion of the area's sunny beaches.
- In New Zealand, the "Kea" bird is known for being mischievous and sometimes stealing tourists' belongings, such as car keys or sunglasses.

- The "Galapagos Islands" are home to the "Flightless Cormorant," a bird that lost its ability to fly due to a lack of natural predators.
- The "Nauru" was once the richest country in the world per capita due to its phosphate deposits, but it has since faced economic challenges.
- The "Hawaiian Islands" have their own time zone, Hawaii-Aleutian Standard Time (HAST), which is 10 hours behind Coordinated Universal Time (UTC-10).
- The "Great Barrier Reef" has a vast range of marine life, including the "Leafy Sea Dragon," which looks like a fantastical creature from a fairy tale.
- The "Australian Coat of Arms" features a kangaroo and an emu because both animals cannot walk backward, symbolizing the country's forward progress.
- In the "Marshall Islands," there is a legend about the "Giant Eel" named "Nareau," which was responsible for creating the islands.
- "Rip currents" in Australia are locally known as "Rips" and are the cause of most surf beach rescues.
- New Zealand's "Whanganui River" was legally recognized as a person by the government in 2017, granting it the same rights as a citizen.
- The "Norfolk Island Pine" is not a pine tree at all but belongs to the family Araucariaceae.
- In "Samoa," tattooing is a highly respected art form, and the traditional tattoo tool is made from boar's teeth.
- The "Rock Islands" in Palau are known for their unique mushroom-shaped limestone islets, providing a picturesque backdrop for diving and snorkeling.
- Australia's "Coober Pedy" is known for its underground churches, where residents can escape the heat while attending mass.
- "Palau" issues the world's first official legal tender coin made of pure silver shaped like a scallop.
- The "Bay of Islands" in New Zealand has exactly 144 islands, despite its name.
- In "Tonga," it is considered bad luck to present someone with a fishing net that has no holes.
- Australia's "Pink Lake" near Esperance in Western Australia owes its pink color to the presence of a certain type of algae.

- "Tahiti" in French Polynesia has a traditional sport called "Ava Tauati," where participants climb coconut trees using their bare hands and feet.
- The "Vava'u Islands" in Tonga are known as the "Whale Watching Capital of the South Pacific" due to their frequent humpback whale sightings.
- "Vanuatu" has the world's only "Post Office Underwater," where divers can post waterproof postcards.
- The "Vaka" canoes of "Cook Islands" have unique triangular sails, similar to those used by ancient Polynesian navigators.
- In "Fiji," the concept of "Tabu" (or "Taboo") involves respecting certain areas or practices considered sacred or restricted.
- The "Solomon Islands" were once known as the "Isles of Solomon" due to the mistaken belief that they were the source of King Solomon's wealth.
- "Kava" is a traditional drink in "Vanuatu" and "Fiji" made from the roots of the kava plant, known for its calming and relaxing effects.
- Australia's "Karijini National Park" has a unique geological feature called "Hancock Gorge," where visitors can hike through narrow and scenic gorges.
- The "Waitangi Treaty Grounds" in New Zealand is the site where the Treaty of Waitangi was signed between the Māori and the British Crown in 1840.
- "Pohnpei" in Micronesia is home to the ancient city of "Nan Madol," a complex of stone structures built on artificial islets in the lagoon.
- The "Hawaiian Hula Dance" was once banned in the 19th century by Christian missionaries who deemed it as sinful.
- The "Snake Gourd" in Oceania is often grown for decorative purposes due to its long and twisted shape.
- "Palau" is home to the world's first and only "Jellyfish Lake," where thousands of non-stinging jellyfish can be safely swum with.
- The "Black Swan" is native to Australia and is the state emblem of Western Australia.
- In "Tonga," it is a tradition to greet someone by sticking out the tongue, known as "tupenu," as a sign of respect.

- The "Hobbit" and "Lord of the Rings" trilogies were filmed entirely in New Zealand, showcasing the country's stunning landscapes.
- Australia's "Kangaroo Island" is also home to the rare "Kangaroo Island Echidna," a type of spiny anteater.
- The "Big Prawn" in Ballina, Australia, is a giant statue of a prawn, celebrating the town's prawn fishing industry.
- The "Tuvalu" uses its unique .tv internet domain to generate income, as it is popular among television broadcasters and video-sharing platforms.
- The "Blue Lagoon" in "Fiji" is a popular attraction for visitors to experience the bright turquoise waters.
- The "Gilbert Islands" in Kiribati are named after Thomas Gilbert, a British captain who sighted the islands in 1788.
- Australia's "Coral Bay" is known for its friendly "Tawny Nurse Sharks," who often swim close to shore.
- The "Whangarei" in New Zealand holds an annual "Sculpture Symposium," where artists create sculptures in public spaces.
- "Micronesian Navigation" relies on reading ocean currents, the stars, and other natural cues to navigate vast distances without instruments.
- Australia's "Great Barrier Reef" is so large that it can be seen from space.
- The "Hawaiian Luau" is a traditional feast where a whole pig is cooked in an underground oven known as an "imu."
- "Kava" ceremonies in "Vanuatu" and "Fiji" involve drinking a traditional beverage made from the root of the kava plant to promote social bonding.
- In "Tahiti," the traditional dance form of "Ori Tahiti" is performed during celebrations, festivals, and even competitions.
- The "Cocos Keeling Islands" in Australia are home to the "Clunies-Ross family," who once owned the entire territory as a private fiefdom.
- "Noumea," the capital of New Caledonia, is nicknamed the "Paris of the Pacific" for its French influence and architecture.
- The "Bora Bora" island in "French Polynesia" was used as a U.S. military supply base during World War II.
- Australia's "Wave Rock" in Western Australia appears like a giant surfing wave in the middle of the outback.
- The "Marquesas Islands" in French Polynesia are famous for their intricate and impressive stone sculptures.

- "Samoans" have a traditional method of tattooing called "Tatau," which covers large portions of the body.
- Australia's "King Island" is known for its world-class dairy products, including its unique "King Island Brie."
- The "Makatea" in French Polynesia is an uplifted coral atoll, forming a raised limestone plateau.
- The "Kilauea" volcano in Hawaii has been erupting continuously since 1983.
- In "New Caledonia," nickel mining is a significant industry, accounting for a large portion of the world's nickel supply.
- The "Tongan Pa'anga" currency depicts various marine life, including whales and turtles.
- "Bounty Day" in "Norfolk Island" is a public holiday commemorating the arrival of the HMS Bounty mutineers on the island in 1856.
- The "Tahitian Garden Eel" is a fascinating creature that buries itself in the sand, leaving only its head visible.
- "Kangaroo Island" in Australia is home to the "Little Sahara," a large area of sand dunes suitable for sandboarding.
- In "Kiribati," the line that marks the International Date Line is named the "Kiribati Line."
- The "Tiare Apetahi" flower in "Tahiti" only blooms for a few hours during early mornings and is considered sacred by the locals.
- The "Lord Howe Island Stick Insect" was once thought to be extinct but was rediscovered on Lord Howe Island in 2001.
- Australia's "Ball's Pyramid" is a unique volcanic rock formation and home to the world's rarest insect, the "Dryococelus australis" or "Lord Howe Island Stick Insect."
- The "Bislama" language in "Vanuatu" uses the word "plastik" to refer to plastic items and has become part of everyday vocabulary.
- "Pohnpei" in Micronesia is home to ancient ruins of "Nan Madol," which is sometimes referred to as the "Venice of the Pacific."
- Australia's "Christmas Island" is home to a unique species of crabs that migrate to the ocean en masse during the rainy season.
- The "Manus Island" in Papua New Guinea is home to ancient "Lapita Pottery," one of the earliest forms of pottery in the Pacific.

- The "Gizo" in "Solomon Islands" is famous for its world-class diving and the "Kennedy Island," where John F. Kennedy once stranded.
- The "Black Pearls" of "Tahiti" are a valuable export, known for their natural beauty and unique color.
- The "Rapa Nui" people of "Easter Island" have a traditional dance called the "Sau Sau," performed during special events and ceremonies.
- Australia's "Great Keppel Island" is home to the "Keppel Bay Sailing Club," one of the oldest yacht clubs in Australia.
- "Kirimati" or "Christmas Island" is the first place in the world to experience the sunrise on Christmas Day.
- In "Micronesia," "Nan Madol" is a megalithic city built on 92 small artificial islets linked by a network of canals.
- "Norfolk Island" has a unique breed of miniature cows, known as "Norfolk Reds."
- The "Anzac Biscuit" in Australia and New Zealand was originally baked by wives and women's groups and sent to soldiers during World War I.
- The "Sky Tower" in "Auckland, New Zealand," is the tallest free-standing structure in the Southern Hemisphere.
- In "Palau," there is a unique swimming spot called "Jellyfish Lake," where visitors can swim with thousands of harmless jellyfish.
- The "Waitangi Treaty Grounds" in New Zealand is home to the world's largest ceremonial war canoe, known as "Ngatokimatawhaorua."
- "Haida Gwaii," formerly known as the "Queen Charlotte Islands," is an archipelago in Canada, but its southernmost islands are located in Oceania.
- "Pohnpei" in Micronesia is home to "Pwudoi," one of the world's most extensive archaeological sites.
- The "Wallis and Futuna Islands" have unique dance performances, such as "Kailao" and "Me'etu'upaki," which are both traditional and competitive.
- "Tuvalu" is one of the world's smallest countries, and its highest point is only about 4.6 meters above sea level.
- "Samoa" is one of the first places in the world to see the sunrise on any given day.
- The "Palm Cockatoo" found in Australia is known for using sticks as drumsticks to create rhythmic beats on trees.

- In "Fiji," locals commonly use "Gong" instead of a bell in schools and churches.
- The "Heilala Festival" in "Tonga" celebrates the country's national flower, the "Heilala," which is a type of gardenia.
- The "Big Bogan" in Nyngan, Australia, is a giant statue of a bogan, a colloquial term for an Australian subculture.
- "Cook Islands Maori" is one of the official languages of "New Zealand."
- "Nauru" once had a thriving phosphate mining industry, but its resources were depleted, leading to environmental and economic challenges.
- The "Tiwi Islands" in Australia have the highest proportion of artists per capita in the country.
- The "Weta" insect found in New Zealand is one of the heaviest insects in the world and is often mistaken for a small mouse.
- In "Tonga," the traditional sport of "Longo" involves men competing to outrun a hurricane.
- "Papua New Guinea" has over 850 distinct languages, making it one of the most linguistically diverse countries globally.
- The "Mudmen" of "Papua New Guinea" wear eerie masks and paint themselves with clay to resemble spirits during traditional rituals.
- In "Vanuatu," land diving is a traditional activity where men jump from tall wooden towers with vines tied to their ankles.
- The "Giant Gippsland Earthworm" found in Australia is the largest species of earthworm in the world and can grow up to 3 meters in length.
- "Bora Bora" in "French Polynesia" has a traditional dance called "Aparima," which tells stories through graceful hand movements.
- The "Kokoda Trail" in "Papua New Guinea" is a challenging trek that follows the route of a significant World War II campaign.
- In "Norfolk Island," it is a tradition to wave at every passing car, as the locals are friendly and known for their warm hospitality.
- The "Rotuman" people of "Fiji" have a traditional dance called "'Apa," which involves precise movements and storytelling.
- "Tasmanian Tigers" had a unique marsupial pouch that faced backward, which scientists believe may have allowed them to hop while running.

- In "Tonga," the "Tupakapakanava" is a ceremonial club that weighs up to 100 pounds and is used during traditional ceremonies.
- "Australia's Rabbit-Proof Fence" was built in the early 20th century to protect crops from rabbits, but some sections are now historical landmarks.
- The "Kiwi" bird in New Zealand has nostrils located at the tip of its long beak, allowing it to sniff out food underground.
- "Nauru" is the third-smallest country in the world by land area, after Vatican City and Monaco.
- The "Solomon Islands" have a traditional sport called "Sika," which involves using a slingshot to propel stones accurately.
- The "Waimea Canyon" in Hawaii, USA, is often referred to as the "Grand Canyon of the Pacific" due to its stunning geological features.
- "Papua New Guinea" has a rich artistic heritage, and the "National Museum and Art Gallery" in Port Moresby houses an extensive collection of traditional art.
- The "Makatea" in French Polynesia is famous for its vast limestone caves, many of which contain hidden waterfalls.
- The "Eugenia Bathurstiana" tree, found in Australia, is so rare that it was once believed to be extinct for over 100 years until it was rediscovered in 1978.
- The "Torres Strait Islanders" in Australia have a traditional dance called the "Tin Dance," which is performed during special occasions.
- "Tuvalu" issues unique .tv internet domain names, making it a source of income for the country.
- The "Rottnest Island" in Australia is home to the "Quokka," a small marsupial known for its friendly and smiling appearance.
- In "Samoa," there is a traditional sport called "Moli," where participants slide down natural water slides created by volcanic rock formations.
- The "Cook Islands" are one of the few countries in the world to use a "roundabout" as a traffic control system.
- The "New Guinea Singing Dog" is a rare and elusive breed of dog, known for its unique vocalizations that resemble singing.
- In "Tonga," it is customary to wear a "Tupenu" wrap skirt, which has different patterns and colors to indicate a person's social status.

- The "Lake Hillier" in Australia has pink-colored water due to the presence of a particular type of algae.
- The "Palau Jellyfish Lake" is home to millions of harmless jellyfish, which have evolved without stinging cells due to the lack of predators.
- "Micronesian Islanders" have a traditional way of preserving food called "umukai," where food is cooked using hot stones and covered with leaves.
- The "Wallis and Futuna Islands" have a unique style of dance called the "Kailao," where dancers use clubs and drums to perform.
- Australia's "Twelve Apostles" on the Great Ocean Road were once known as the "Sow and Piglets" before the erosion changed their appearance.
- In "Nauru," there is a popular sport called "Te Aka," which involves throwing a large stick as far as possible.
- The "Samoa Scops Owl" is one of the smallest owl species in the world and is found only in Samoa.
- The "Blackfooted Rock Wallaby" in Australia is known for its impressive climbing skills and can leap up to 10 feet from a standing position.
- In "Tahiti," the traditional "Otea" dance is performed by both men and women, featuring fast hip shaking movements.
- Australia's "Pink Lake Hillier" is particularly vibrant in color during the hottest months of the year.
- The "Tongan Fruit Bat" is the national animal of "Tonga" and is also known as the "Flying Fox" due to its large wingspan.
- The "Ulupalakua Ranch" in Hawaii is home to the world's largest dormant volcano, "Haleakalā."
- In "Vanuatu," there is a traditional practice called "Nambas," where men wear penis sheaths made from the leaves of the pandanus tree.
- The "Hauraki Gulf" near Auckland, New Zealand, is home to the world's smallest and rarest dolphin, the "Maui Dolphin."
- "Nauru" is one of the few countries without an official capital city, and its largest city, Yaren, serves as the de facto capital.
- The "Rioli" family of "Tiwi Islands" in Australia has produced several talented Australian Rules football players.
- The "Yapese" people of "Micronesia" use large stone discs called "Rai stones" as a form of currency, despite not using them for daily transactions anymore.

- The "Coconut Crab" found in "Kiribati" and other Pacific islands is the world's largest terrestrial arthropod.
- In "Samoa," traditional tattoo artists, called "Tufuga ta tatau," use handmade tools to perform intricate tatau (tattoo) designs.
- The "Tangaroa" in Maori mythology is the god of the sea and oceans.
- The "Giant Kauri Snail" in "New Zealand" is one of the world's largest land snails and is endangered due to habitat loss.
- "Niue" has a one-of-a-kind coin collection that features popular Disney characters, making them sought-after collector's items.
- In "Kiribati," Christmas celebrations are extended to the entire month of December, with each village taking turns to host the festivities.
- The "Australian Coat of Arms" features a kangaroo and an emu, as both animals are unable to walk backward, symbolizing progress.
- The "Talai" in "Tuvalu" is a traditional method of apology, where the person seeking forgiveness crawls under the legs of the offended party.
- In "Fiji," there is a traditional ceremony called "Vaka Eke," where a new canoe is launched with a festive celebration.
- The "Kava" ceremony in "Vanuatu" is a solemn ritual that requires participants to clap once before and after drinking the traditional beverage.
- The "Great Keppel Island" in Australia is known for its pristine beaches and is often referred to as the "Jewel of the Southern Great Barrier Reef."
- In "Papua New Guinea," the "Kina" is the official currency and is named after the native word for the shell of the "Penis clam."
- The "Lapita" pottery in "New Caledonia" and other Pacific islands is named after the archaeological site where it was first discovered.
- Australia's "Fraser Island" is the largest sand island in the world and has over 100 freshwater lakes.
- The "Rotuman" language in "Fiji" has no swear words, making it a polite and respectful culture.
- The "Caroline Island" in "Kiribati" was the first place on Earth to experience the new millennium in the year 2000.
- The "Māori haka" performed by the "New Zealand All Blacks" rugby team was traditionally used to intimidate enemies but is now performed to honor opponents.

- The "Palau Track and Field Association" uses "jellyfish" as their mascot, symbolizing endurance and strength.
- In "Samoa," there is a tradition of naming babies after the day of the week they are born on.
- The "Solomon Islands" have a unique aeroplane taxi service, where small planes are used to transport people between islands.
- Australia's "Lord Howe Island" is home to the "Kurtome" spider, the world's smallest known spider.
- "New Caledonia" is home to the "Kagu," a flightless bird with beautiful plumage and unique courtship displays.
- The "Tahitian Black Pearls" are known for their rare and stunning colors, ranging from dark green to peacock blue.
- "Aloha" is a Hawaiian word that means both "hello" and "goodbye."
- In "Kiribati," the traditional sport of "te noero" involves dancing on the surface of the water.
- "Rapa Nui" or "Easter Island" got its name because it was discovered by Dutch explorer Jacob Roggeveen on Easter Sunday in 1722.
- The "Tongan pa'anga" is the world's heaviest coin, weighing 1 kilogram and worth around 5,000 pa'anga.
- In "Fiji," the "Bouma Falls" are said to be the bathing place of gods and spirits.
- Australia's "Coober Pedy" has unique underground churches due to the extreme heat on the surface.
- The "Niuean" language uses the word "aloof" to describe the feeling of contentment after eating a satisfying meal.
- "Papua New Guinea" has over 700 bird species, making it one of the world's most biodiverse countries for avian life.
- In "Tahiti," traditional dances are accompanied by "To'ere" drums, made from hollowed-out tree trunks.
- The "Banzai Pipeline" in Hawaii is one of the world's most famous surf spots, known for its massive waves.
- The "Maori haka" performed by the "New Zealand All Blacks" rugby team has different versions for various occasions, each with a specific meaning.
- "Christmas Island" in Australia is famous for its annual migration of millions of red crabs.
- The "Samoan slap dance" is a dance form that involves dancers slapping different parts of their bodies rhythmically.

- "New Zealand" has more sheep than people, making it one of the highest sheep-to-human ratios in the world.
- In "Vanuatu," it is customary to give a small gift when entering someone's home.
- The "Elcho Island" in Australia is home to the Yolngu people, who are known for their vibrant and intricate artwork.
- The "Wallis and Futuna Islands" are the only French territory to use its flag alongside the French flag.
- "Mount Kosciuszko" in Australia is the highest mountain on the Australian mainland.
- "Tonga" is one of the few countries in the world to have never been colonized.
- The "Ni-Vanuatu" people believe that spirits exist in natural objects like rocks and trees.
- The "Tiwi Islands" in Australia have one of the highest percentages of artists per population in the world.
- "Nauru" is the third-smallest country by population, with around 10,000 residents.
- The "Coconut Palm" is often referred to as the "Tree of Life" because it can provide food, water, shelter, and various materials.
- "Micronesian Stick Chart" is a traditional navigational tool used by "Micronesian Islanders" to navigate the open ocean.
- "Vanuatu" has the world's highest density of languages per capita, with over 130 indigenous languages spoken.
- The "Rotuman" people of "Fiji" celebrate "Rotuma Day" on May 13 each year to honor their culture and history.
- In "Papua New Guinea," locals create art using "Bilum," a traditional woven bag.
- The "Black Sand Beaches" of "Hawaii" get their color from the volcanic activity in the region.
- "Fiji" has a tradition of welcoming visitors with a "Kava Ceremony," where a traditional drink is shared.
- The "Otago Gold Rush" in "New Zealand" attracted thousands of prospectors in the 1860s.
- "The Thorny Devil" is a unique lizard species found in Australia, known for its spiky appearance.
- The "Nasal Moka" is a traditional exchange of gifts among the "Trobriand Islanders" in "Papua New Guinea."

Chapter 7: Antarctica

- Antarctica is the southernmost continent and the fifth largest, covering an area of 14 million square kilometers (5.4 million square miles).
- It is the coldest, windiest, and driest continent on Earth.
- The highest temperature ever recorded on Antarctica was 20.75 degrees Celsius (69.35 degrees Fahrenheit).
- The Antarctic Peninsula is one of the fastest-warming regions globally, experiencing significant climate change.
- Antarctica contains approximately 70% of the world's freshwater in the form of ice.
- The continent is surrounded by the Southern Ocean, which is the fourth-largest ocean.
- There is no official time zone in Antarctica, but research stations often use the time zone of the country they are owned by.
- Emperor penguins are the largest and heaviest of all penguin species and are native to Antarctica.
- Antarctica is home to the only active volcano on the continent, Mount Erebus.

- The coldest temperature ever recorded on Earth was -128.6 degrees Celsius (-199.5 degrees Fahrenheit) at Antarctica's Dome Fuji station.
- Antarctica is the only continent without a native human population.
- The only permanent residents of Antarctica are scientists and researchers from various countries.
- The international Antarctic Treaty, signed in 1959, designates Antarctica as a scientific preserve and bans military activity on the continent.
- The South Pole is located in Antarctica, where all lines of longitude converge.
- There are no native land mammals on the continent. The wildlife consists mainly of marine species and birds.
- The Weddell Sea is known for its frequent formation of colossal icebergs.
- Antarctica is the largest desert in the world, with very little precipitation.
- Lake Vostok, buried beneath the ice, is one of the largest subglacial lakes in Antarctica.
- Adélie penguins are named after the wife of French explorer Jules Dumont d'Urville.
- Some parts of Antarctica receive no sunlight for several months during winter, while others experience constant daylight during summer.
- The Dry Valleys are one of the driest places on Earth, receiving almost no snow or ice accumulation.
- In 1979, Antarctica's Mount Erebus had the first-ever commercial airline flight over the continent.
- A research station called "Villa Las Estrellas" has a civilian population, mainly consisting of families of Chilean military personnel.
- The Soviet Union's "Vostok Station" recorded the lowest temperature ever measured on Earth.
- The "Don Juan Pond" in Antarctica is the saltiest body of water on Earth, even saltier than the Dead Sea.
- The first person to set foot on Antarctica was the American explorer John Davis in 1821.
- A famous explorer who disappeared while exploring Antarctica is Sir Ernest Shackleton.

- The Antarctic Ice Sheet is almost 5 kilometers (3 miles) thick in some areas.
- The world's first-ever entirely wind-powered research station is the "Princess Elisabeth Station" in Antarctica.
- Antarctica contains around 90% of the world's ice and 70% of its freshwater.
- The ozone hole, an area of significant ozone depletion, was discovered over Antarctica in the 1980s.
- The "McMurdo Station" in Antarctica is the largest research station on the continent.
- The "Antarctic Peninsula" is one of the most rapidly warming regions globally, with temperature rises exceeding the global average.
- In the summer months, the population on Antarctica can exceed 5,000 people, but it dramatically drops during winter.
- Antarctic krill are small, shrimp-like creatures that are a vital part of the food chain in the Southern Ocean.
- The "Ross Ice Shelf" in Antarctica is the largest floating ice shelf in the world.
- The "Transantarctic Mountains" divide East Antarctica from West Antarctica.
- Some icebergs in Antarctica can be larger than entire countries.
- "Port Lockroy" is a former British research station that now operates as a museum and post office for tourists.
- The "Ellsworth Mountains" in Antarctica are the highest mountain range in the continent.
- Antarctic snow can appear pink or red due to the presence of microorganisms called "snow algae."
- "The Antarctic Circle" is an imaginary line located at approximately 66.5 degrees south latitude.
- The "Bellingshausen Station" in Antarctica is named after the Russian explorer Fabian Gottlieb Thaddeus von Bellingshausen.
- Antarctica's subglacial lakes contain unique ecosystems that may provide insights into life on other planets.
- The "Amundsen-Scott South Pole Station" is one of the primary research stations located at the South Pole.
- Scientists have discovered ancient fossils in Antarctica, indicating that the continent was once warmer and covered in forests.
- "Ellsworth Land" in Antarctica is named after Lincoln Ellsworth, an American polar explorer.

- The "Antarctic Convergence" is a meeting point of different ocean currents, which helps to isolate Antarctica climatically.
- "Antarctic Sound" is a body of water known for its stunning icebergs and frequently visited by tourists.
- Antarctica's ice sheets contain enough water to raise global sea levels by approximately 58 meters (190 feet) if they were to melt entirely.
- The "Penguin Post Office" in Port Lockroy is the most popular tourist destination in Antarctica.
- Emperor penguins are known for their exceptional diving abilities, reaching depths of up to 550 meters (1,800 feet) to find food.
- The "Wandering Albatross" has the largest wingspan of any bird on Earth, reaching up to 3.7 meters (12 feet).
- Icefish found in Antarctic waters have blood that lacks hemoglobin, making it transparent.
- The "Amundsen Sea" in Antarctica is named after the famous Norwegian explorer Roald Amundsen.
- Despite its harsh conditions, certain mosses, lichens, and algae manage to survive on the Antarctic Peninsula.
- Antarctica has no permanent rivers; however, glacial meltwater forms temporary streams during the summer.
- "The Argentine Primavera Base" is the world's southernmost art gallery, featuring works from Argentine artists.
- A famous landmark known as "Inaccessible Island" in South Georgia and the South Sandwich Islands is ironically named.
- "Palmer Station" in Antarctica is the only U.S. research station that operates year-round.
- Researchers from various countries conduct cutting-edge scientific research in Antarctica, including climate studies and astronomy.
- Despite its remote location, Antarctica is vulnerable to pollution and waste due to human activities.
- Whales, such as humpback and killer whales, migrate to Antarctic waters during the summer to feed on krill.
- The continent experiences "whiteouts," where the bright white snow and clouds blend together, causing a loss of visibility.
- The "Antarctic Treaty System" prohibits any military activity on the continent and promotes international cooperation in research.

- The first woman to set foot on Antarctica was Caroline Mikkelsen, a Norwegian explorer's wife, in 1935.
- The "South Orkney Islands" are located at the entrance to the Weddell Sea, making them an essential research location.
- Antarctica has no native reptiles or amphibians.
- The "Yamato Mountains" in Antarctica are the highest mountains on the continent.
- The "Antarctic ice sheet" contains around 70% of the world's freshwater.
- Antarctica has a significant impact on Earth's climate, as its ice reflects sunlight back into space.
- Despite its extreme cold, Antarctica has experienced rare instances of rain.
- The "Ross Ice Shelf" is an enormous floating ice shelf named after British explorer James Clark Ross.
- Antarctica's remoteness and cold temperatures have made it an ideal location for testing space exploration equipment.
- The Soviet Union's "Vostok Station" recorded the coldest temperature ever measured on Earth, at -89.2 degrees Celsius (-128.6 degrees Fahrenheit).
- The "Adélie Land Meteorite" is the largest meteorite ever found in Antarctica, weighing over 1.4 metric tons.
- The "Byrd Glacier" in Antarctica is one of the world's fastest-moving glaciers.
- The "Ronne Ice Shelf" is one of the largest ice shelves in Antarctica, named after American explorer Finn Ronne.
- Weddell seals are known for their exceptional diving abilities, reaching depths of up to 600 meters (1,970 feet).
- The "Mertz Glacier Tongue" collapsed in 2010, creating an iceberg twice the size of Luxembourg.
- The "Amery Ice Shelf" in Antarctica is one of the largest ice shelves in the world.
- Scientists have found fossilized dinosaur bones in Antarctica, indicating the continent was once warmer and inhabited by dinosaurs.
- The "Antarctic Petrel" is a seabird native to Antarctica and surrounding waters.
- The "Polar Plateau" in Antarctica is one of the most desolate and isolated regions on Earth.
- Scientists study ice cores from Antarctica to gain insights into past climate conditions and atmospheric composition.

- Antarctica is a hub for important research in astrophysics due to its pristine and dry air, ideal for stargazing.
- The "Mawson Station" in Antarctica is Australia's oldest research station, established in 1954.
- The "Bellingshausen Sea" is named after Russian explorer Fabian Gottlieb Thaddeus von Bellingshausen.
- The "Antarctic Circumpolar Current" is the world's strongest ocean current, circulating around Antarctica.
- Antarctica is home to unique ice formations, such as "ice shelves" and "tabular icebergs."
- The "Gamburtsev Mountains" in Antarctica are hidden beneath thick ice and were only discovered in the 1950s.
- The "Amundsen-Scott South Pole Station" has an annual marathon where participants run in temperatures well below freezing.
- The "Antarctic Hairgrass" is one of the only flowering plants native to Antarctica.
- Penguins often slide on their bellies, a behavior called "tobogganing," to conserve energy while traveling across ice.
- The "Transantarctic Mountains" are among the longest mountain ranges on Earth, stretching over 3,500 kilometers (2,175 miles).
- The "Palmer Archipelago" in Antarctica is a haven for marine life, including seals, whales, and penguins.
- Due to its harsh conditions, many early explorers who ventured to Antarctica faced extreme hardships and perished.
- The "Antarctic Peninsula" is the northernmost part of the continent and the most accessible for visitors.
- The "Erebus Ice Tongue" in Antarctica is a floating glacier tongue named after the famous ship, HMS Erebus.
- Antarctica's vast ice sheets contain an estimated 90% of the world's ice and about 70% of the planet's freshwater.
- The "McMurdo Dry Valleys" in Antarctica are the driest place on Earth, with very little snow or ice cover.
- Antarctica has no native trees or woody plants.
- The "Deception Island" in Antarctica is a volcanic island with a natural harbor known as "Neptune's Bellows."
- The "Ron Hubbard Range" in Antarctica is named after the famous science fiction writer L. Ron Hubbard.

- "IceCube Neutrino Observatory" in Antarctica is a research facility studying neutrinos, high-energy particles from outer space.
- A "tabular iceberg" is a type of iceberg with a flat top and steep sides, often several kilometers long.
- Antarctica has no reptiles or amphibians, but it is home to many species of seabirds and seals.
- The "Antarctic Fur Seal" is one of the only two mammals native to Antarctica, the other being the Weddell seal.
- Antarctica is considered a desert due to its low precipitation levels, with some areas receiving less than 2 inches of precipitation per year.
- The "Balleny Islands" in Antarctica are a group of sub-Antarctic islands named after John Balleny, a British explorer.
- The "Antarctic Peninsula" has been experiencing some of the most rapid warming on the continent.
- The "Southern Ocean" surrounding Antarctica is known for its powerful and continuous "westerly winds."
- Antarctica is approximately twice the size of Australia.
- "Antarctic icefish" have evolved to have clear blood and no red blood cells, enabling them to survive in icy waters.
- The "Antarctic Blue Whale" is the largest animal on Earth, with lengths reaching up to 100 feet.
- The "Prince Edward Islands" in Antarctica are a group of sub-Antarctic islands known for their diverse wildlife.
- The "Wilkes Land" in Antarctica is an area of the continent claimed by Australia.
- "Antarctic krill" is a small, shrimp-like creature that forms the base of the Antarctic food chain.
- The "Weddell Sea" in Antarctica is named after British sailor James Weddell.
- Antarctica is the least populated continent, with only a few thousand people during the summer research season.
- The "South Pole Telescope" in Antarctica is used to study cosmic microwave background radiation.
- Antarctica has no active volcanoes, although there are extinct and dormant volcanoes on the continent.
- The "Antarctic Toothfish" is a large predatory fish found in the Southern Ocean.
- The "Palmer Deep" off the Antarctic Peninsula is one of the deepest oceanic trenches in the world.

- The "Penguin Highway" in Antarctica refers to penguin trails leading from colonies to the ocean.
- The "Aurora Australis" is a stunning natural light display in the Southern Hemisphere, similar to the Northern Lights.
- The "Cosmonauts Sea" in Antarctica is named after the Russian space program.
- "McMurdo Station" in Antarctica has its own post office, allowing visitors to send mail with a unique Antarctic postmark.
- The "Antarctic Sound" is a narrow body of water known for its large icebergs and scenic views.
- "Mount Erebus" in Antarctica is the world's southernmost active volcano.
- Antarctica is the world's largest desert, despite being covered in ice.
- The "Weddell seal" is known for its unique vocalizations and can dive to depths of over 600 meters (1,970 feet).
- The "Katabatic winds" in Antarctica are strong, cold winds that flow from the interior to the coast.
- The "McMurdo Sound" in Antarctica is famous for being the location of "Discovery Hut," an early Antarctic base.
- Scientists have discovered meteorites in Antarctica, brought to the surface by glacial movements.
- The "Challenger Deep" in the Antarctic Ocean is one of the world's deepest ocean trenches.
- Antarctica's ice is so heavy that it has caused the land beneath it to sink.
- The "Gough Island" in Antarctica is a UNESCO World Heritage Site known for its seabird colonies.
- The "Antarctic Circumpolar Current" connects the Atlantic, Indian, and Pacific Oceans, flowing around Antarctica.
- "Elephant Island" in Antarctica is named after the elephant seals that inhabit the area.
- The "Adélie Coast" in Antarctica is a region named after the wife of French explorer Jules Dumont d'Urville.
- The "Drake Passage" between South America and Antarctica is known for its turbulent waters.
- Antarctica has unique microorganisms called "extremophiles" that can survive in extreme conditions.
- "Dome Argus" in Antarctica is one of the coldest places on Earth, with temperatures reaching below -80 degrees Celsius.

- The "Gulf Stream" carries warm water to the coast of Antarctica, affecting its climate.
- The "Australian Antarctic Territory" is one of the seven claims to Antarctic territory.
- The "Antarctic Convergence" is an area where cold Antarctic waters meet warmer sub-Antarctic waters.
- Antarctica is the only continent with no commercial airports.
- "Mawson's Huts" in Antarctica are historic structures used during Douglas Mawson's expedition.
- The "Antarctic Snow Cruiser" was a massive vehicle designed for exploration, but it proved impractical and was abandoned.
- Emperor penguins have a unique adaptation called "brood pouch," where the males keep the eggs warm during incubation.
- The "Adélie Penguin" is named after the wife of Jules Dumont d'Urville, a French explorer.
- The "Australian Antarctic Division" conducts research and operates research stations in Antarctica.
- The "Mount Erebus" volcano in Antarctica has an active lava lake inside its crater.
- Icebergs can sometimes flip over, exposing their submerged sections above water.
- Antarctica is a hotbed for studying climate change due to its sensitivity to global warming.
- The "Antarctic Prion" is a small seabird found in the Southern Ocean.
- The "Ross Dependency" in Antarctica is a New Zealand territory claimed in 1923.
- The "Antarctic Specially Protected Areas" (ASPA) are designated regions to protect specific scientific, environmental, and historic values.
- The "South Shetland Islands" in Antarctica are a group of sub-Antarctic islands that are important for wildlife conservation.
- Antarctica has unique geological formations called "nunataks," which are exposed mountain peaks surrounded by ice.
- The "Aurora australis" is the Southern Hemisphere's counterpart to the Northern Lights.
- Antarctica is the only continent where humans have no traditional inhabitants or indigenous people.
- Some research stations in Antarctica use renewable energy sources like wind and solar power.

- The "Larsen Ice Shelf" in Antarctica is known for its dramatic calving events, where large icebergs break off.
- The "McMurdo Station" in Antarctica has an annual music festival called "IceStock."
- The "Bouvet Island" in Antarctica is one of the most remote and uninhabited places on Earth.
- Whales, seals, and penguins in Antarctica communicate underwater using a variety of sounds.
- The "Ronne-Filchner Ice Shelf" is one of the largest ice shelves in Antarctica, named after its discoverers.
- Antarctica has been used as a location for filming documentaries and movies due to its unique landscape.
- Some bacteria found in Antarctic ice may have medical applications, such as producing antibiotics.
- The "Petermann Glacier" in Antarctica is one of the largest floating ice tongues.
- The "Australian Antarctic Program" conducts research on Antarctica and the Southern Ocean.
- The "Amundsen-Scott South Pole Station" celebrates "Winter Solstice" with a traditional feast in the dark winter months.
- "Aurora Research" in Antarctica involves studying the Earth's magnetosphere and its interaction with solar wind.
- The "Southern Ocean" surrounding Antarctica is known for its rich marine biodiversity, including many species of whales.
- Some icebergs in Antarctica can be massive, reaching sizes of more than 10 times the size of Manhattan.
- The "Mendel Polar Station" in Antarctica is a Czech research station named after Gregor Mendel, the father of modern genetics.
- Antarctica is home to ancient meteorites that provide valuable insights into the history of our solar system.
- The "Antarctic Plate" is a tectonic plate underlying the continent of Antarctica.
- The "Dry Valleys" in Antarctica are so arid that ice can sublimate directly into vapor without melting.
- Some icebergs in Antarctica can be bizarre shapes, resembling animals, people, or objects.
- The "Amery Ice Shelf" in Antarctica is one of the largest ice shelves in the world.
- The "Belgian Antarctic Expedition" in 1897 was the first to spend a winter on the continent.

- The "South Orkney Islands" in Antarctica are among the coldest places on Earth.
- Antarctica has no native land insects, but some insects, like flies and beetles, are found in coastal regions.
- "Vostok Station" in Antarctica is famous for drilling deep ice cores, revealing ancient climate records.
- The "Bentley Subglacial Trench" in Antarctica is one of the deepest under-ice locations on Earth.
- The "Orcadas Base" in Antarctica is one of the oldest continuously operating research stations on the continent.
- "Antarctic blue ice" is created when snow is compressed into dense ice, causing air bubbles to be expelled.
- Antarctica is home to a variety of seals, including leopard seals, Weddell seals, and Ross seals.
- The "Princess Elisabeth Station" in Antarctica is the first zero-emission research station powered entirely by renewable energy.
- Antarctica's icebergs can be a stunning turquoise color due to the presence of tiny ice crystals.
- "Antarctic Treaty Consultative Meetings" are held regularly to discuss governance and conservation issues related to Antarctica.
- Some areas in Antarctica receive no rainfall for decades, making them the driest places on Earth.
- Antarctica's remote and pristine environment makes it an important natural laboratory for scientific research and discovery.
- The "Larsen C Ice Shelf" in Antarctica is one of the largest ice shelves on the continent.
- Antarctica is the only continent without a time zone; researchers and visitors often use the time zone of their home country or the time zone of their research station.
- The "Antarctic Treaty" was signed in 1959 and prohibits military activity, nuclear testing, and mineral mining on the continent.
- "Antarctic blue ice runways" are created by bulldozing a layer of snow to expose the blue ice beneath, making it easier for aircraft to land.
- Antarctica's ice contains ancient air bubbles that provide valuable information about past atmospheric conditions.

- The "South Sandwich Islands" in Antarctica are a volcanic island chain that experiences frequent volcanic activity.
- "Lake Vostok" in Antarctica is one of the largest subglacial lakes and has been isolated from the outside world for millions of years.
- Antarctica's ice sheet is so massive that it has a significant effect on the Earth's gravitational field.
- The "Antarctic Geomagnetic Pole" is the point where the Earth's magnetic field is directed vertically downwards.
- Antarctica's icebergs can come in a variety of colors, including white, blue, green, and black.
- The "East Antarctic Ice Sheet" is one of the two main ice sheets on the continent and is the largest in terms of volume.
- Scientists have discovered fossils of ancient marine creatures, including giant marine reptiles and prehistoric sharks, in Antarctica.
- The "South Pole Traverse" is an overland route used by researchers to transport supplies and equipment to the South Pole.
- The "Marie Byrd Land" in Antarctica is named after the wife of American explorer Richard E. Byrd.
- Antarctica's ice sheets are so heavy that they cause the Earth's crust to flex and deform.
- The "Marie Byrd Seamounts" are a group of underwater mountains located off the coast of Marie Byrd Land.
- Antarctica is home to the coldest and windiest places on Earth, including "Dome Fuji," where temperatures can drop below -90 degrees Celsius.
- The "Chilean Antarctic Territory" is one of the seven territorial claims on Antarctica.
- The "Lassiter Coast" in Antarctica is named after a fictional character from the movie "Aliens."
- The "Transantarctic Mountains" are one of the longest mountain ranges on Earth, stretching across the continent.
- Antarctica has a phenomenon called "sea ice extent," where the area of ice-covered ocean fluctuates seasonally.
- The "Antarctic Peninsula" is one of the fastest-warming regions on the planet, with temperatures rising at a rate of nearly 0.5 degrees Celsius per decade.
- The "Antarctic Peninsula" has a higher diversity of bird species than any other region on the continent.

- Antarctica's ice shelves can be subject to "calving," where large sections break off and form icebergs.
- The "Antarctic Geodetic Dome" is a geodetic station used for measuring the Earth's shape and rotation.
- The "Antarctic Sound" is known for its pristine and untouched environment, making it an important ecological region.
- Antarctica has an active volcano named "Mount Sidley," located in the Marie Byrd Land region.
- The "Siple Coast" in Antarctica is named after American physicist Paul Siple, known for his contributions to Antarctic research.
- The "Yamato-1 Glacier" in Antarctica is named after the first Japanese Antarctic research expedition.
- Antarctica is the coldest place on Earth, with the lowest recorded temperature of -89.2 degrees Celsius (-128.6 degrees Fahrenheit).
- The "Amery Ice Shelf" in Antarctica is the third-largest ice shelf on the continent.
- Antarctica's ice is made up of compressed snow that fell thousands of years ago.
- The "Ellsworth Mountains" in Antarctica are one of the highest mountain ranges on the continent.
- The "Antarctic Plateau" is one of the most stable and flat regions on Earth, making it ideal for astronomical observations.
- The "Wilkes Land crater" is a large impact crater buried beneath the ice of East Antarctica.
- Antarctica's ice sheets are constantly moving, flowing towards the coast due to their own weight.
- The "South Pole Telescope" is used to study the cosmic microwave background radiation, providing insights into the early universe.
- The "Australian Antarctic Division" conducts research on wildlife, climate change, and marine ecosystems in Antarctica.
- Antarctica is home to the longest-lived animal on Earth, the "Antarctic sponge" that can live for over 1,500 years.
- The "Antarctic Peninsula" is home to the majority of research stations on the continent.
- The "Antarctic Circle" is an imaginary line at 66.5 degrees south, marking the point where the sun does not rise on the winter solstice.

- Antarctica is the only continent where the government of a country (Chile) operates a civilian settlement, known as "Villa Las Estrellas."
- The "Mount Erebus" volcano has a persistent lava lake, making it one of the few volcanoes with a continuous eruption.
- The "Balleny Islands" in Antarctica are named after John Balleny, a British whaler who discovered them in 1839.
- Antarctica has no permanent residents, only research station staff who stay for varying periods.
- The "Antarctic Blue Ice Runways" are used for aircraft landings because of their firm and stable surface.
- Antarctica's ice contains layers of ancient snow, providing a record of past atmospheric conditions and climate changes.
- The "South Polar Skua" is a bird of prey found in Antarctica known for stealing food from other birds.
- Antarctica is an essential part of the global climate system, influencing ocean circulation and sea level rise.
- The "Antarctic Artists and Writers Program" invites artists and writers to stay in Antarctica and draw inspiration from its unique environment.
- Antarctica is the windiest continent, with some regions experiencing hurricane-force winds.
- The "Ronald Amundsen Memorial" in Antarctica honors the first person to reach the South Pole.
- The "Antarctic Pearlwort" is one of the only two flowering plant species found on the continent.
- The "Antarctic Tern" holds the record for the longest migratory journey of any bird, traveling from Antarctica to the Arctic and back each year.
- The "Ross Sea" in Antarctica is the world's most productive marine ecosystem.
- Antarctica has no permanent rivers or lakes, but it does have seasonal meltwater ponds and streams.
- The "Antarctic Blue Whale" has a heart that weighs as much as a small car and a tongue that can weigh as much as an elephant.
- The "Belgian Antarctic Research Expedition" in 1898 was the first expedition to spend the winter on the continent.
- The "Antarctic Specially Managed Area" (ASMA) is a designation used to manage specific areas of special interest and ecological significance.

- The "Emperor Penguin" is the largest and heaviest of all penguin species, reaching heights of up to 4 feet (1.2 meters).
- Antarctica's icebergs can make eerie sounds, often described as "booming" or "thunderous."
- The "Antarctic Treaty System" has been in effect since 1961 and includes measures to protect the environment and promote scientific cooperation.
- The "Weddell Sea" in Antarctica is known for its extensive ice cover and large population of seals.
- Antarctica's ice sheets can be up to 4.7 kilometers (2.9 miles) thick in some places.
- The "Australian Antarctic Division" operates the "Casey Station," which is one of the largest research stations on the continent.
- Antarctica's ice contains tiny air bubbles that can reveal the atmospheric composition of the past.
- The "Queen Maud Land" in Antarctica is a Norwegian territory claimed in 1939.
- The "Antarctic Sun" is visible for 24 hours a day during the austral summer at the South Pole.
- Antarctica is the only continent that does not have a military presence or defense forces.
- The "Antarctic Desert" is the coldest and driest desert in the world, with little to no precipitation.
- The "Ferrar Glacier" in Antarctica is known for its striking blue ice, caused by compressed snow crystals.
- Antarctica has unique geological features called "glacial erratics," which are large boulders carried by glaciers and left behind as the ice retreats.
- The "International Thwaites Glacier Collaboration" is a research effort to study the Thwaites Glacier and its potential impact on sea-level rise.
- "Antarctic Pearlwort" plants can endure freezing temperatures and strong winds, allowing them to survive in the harsh conditions.
- The "Antarctic Search for Meteorites" program collects meteorites that have fallen to Earth from space.
- Antarctica's ice sheet is so massive that it exerts a gravitational pull, attracting seawater towards it.
- The "Amundsen Sea" in Antarctica is named after Norwegian explorer Roald Amundsen.

- Antarctica's "McMurdo Dry Valleys" have been described as a polar desert, where little precipitation falls.
- The "Marie Byrd Land" region in Antarctica is known for its large volcanic province.
- The "Pine Island Glacier" in Antarctica is one of the fastest-moving glaciers on the continent.
- The "Antarctic Ecosystem" is unique, with many species found nowhere else on Earth.
- Antarctica's ice contains layers that record past volcanic eruptions and dust from distant deserts.
- The "Australian Antarctic Territory" is the largest of the seven territorial claims on the continent.
- Antarctica's ice reflects sunlight, helping to regulate the Earth's temperature.
- The "Antarctic Desert" covers an area of over 14 million square kilometers (5.4 million square miles).
- The "Antarctic Silverfish" is a small fish found in the Southern Ocean.
- The "Amundsen-Scott South Pole Station" is named after Norwegian explorer Roald Amundsen and British explorer Robert F. Scott.
- Antarctica has a unique ecosystem of marine organisms that have adapted to life in the cold, dark waters.
- The "Marie Byrd Seamounts" are a chain of underwater mountains in the Amundsen Sea.
- Antarctica's "Ross Ice Shelf" is the largest ice shelf in the world, covering an area roughly the size of France.
- The "Adelie Land" in Antarctica is a French territory claimed in 1840.
- Antarctica's icebergs can be classified into different shapes, including tabular, wedge, and blocky.

Check out Dr. Leo Lexicon's most
popular release and read an excerpt:

AI for Smart Kids Ages 6-9

WHAT YOU WILL LEARN

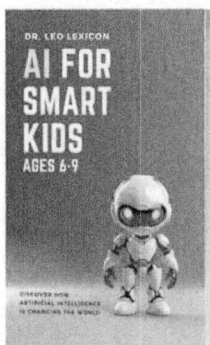

✓ Discover: What is AI and how is it used in everyday life
✓ Explore: From Narrow AI to Super AI, meet AI's real superpowers
✓ Dive into AI history: Meet the Key Inventors, from ancient times to today
✓ Understand: Data, machine learning, and programming, the building blocks of AI
✓ Imagine the future with AI: Education, jobs, creativity, ethics, and beyond. Get involved!

DR. LEO LEXICON

AI FOR SMART KIDS

AGES 6-9

Scan the QR Code to order the book now!

EXCERPT

Chapter 2: The Types of AI

Defining AI

Let us start the chapter by agreeing on how to define AI. We already talked about some examples that show you how AI actually works. In general, when computers are programmed to be extremely intelligent and perform tasks that typically require human intelligence, such as learning, problem-solving, and decision-making, this is known as artificial intelligence, or AI. This is the working definition of AI we will use for the rest of the book.

Typically, we can think of three types of AI: narrow AI, general AI, and super AI. Let us take a look at what we mean by these:

Narrow AI

Narrow AI is comparable to a computer that does well at only one specific task. It is similar to being an expert in a particular task, like understanding Egyptian hieroglyphs, or knowing all about planes, for example. Now consider a computer that is particularly good at playing the game of chess. It is a master chess player who is familiar with all the moves and tactics, and has learned how to play by analyzing thousands, if not millions, of games. However, because it is so focused on chess, if you asked it to do something else, like ride a bicycle or paint a picture, it wouldn't know how to do those things.

Another well-known example is a computer that can scan images and tell you whether a cat is present. This has actually been tried out at top technology companies as a test to see if the AI actually works. This computer can quickly respond, "Yes, there's a cat!" or "No, there isn't!" when you show it a picture because it has been trained to recognize what a cat looks like. However, due to its focus on finding cats, if you asked it to do something else, like tell you if an elephant was present in the image or count the number of trees in another image, it would be unable to do so.

General AI

The next type of AI we will look at is General AI. Now, General AI is similar to having a computer that is extremely intelligent, just like a very smart person. It has a wide range of abilities (as opposed to narrow ones), just like humans do. It can pick up new information, comprehend what it sees, and even perform tasks that we haven't explicitly taught it how to do. So, as you can see, it is quite different from narrow AI.

Think of a friend you have who is very intelligent and versatile. They are capable of telling jokes, playing sports, doing math, and painting stunning works of art. Everything they put their mind to, it seems like they pick up that skill very fast. That is how general AI operates. It can learn from humans and comprehend the knowledge we possess, enabling it to assist us with a variety of tasks.

Say you teach the general AI how to play the game of chess. Like the narrow AI whom we met earlier and who was an expert at playing chess, the general AI will pick up the game and get really good at it. The interesting part is that the general AI can also pick up other games like checkers or tic-tac-toe without having been explicitly taught those games. It can learn how to play new games by applying the knowledge it already possesses and using its powers of observation and analysis.

General AI is also capable of human-like comprehension. It can be taught to recognize various objects, animals, and even the definitions of words and sentences. It can therefore perform many tasks just like us and is comparable to a really smart computer friend. Even though we haven't taught it yet, it is capable of learning, comprehending, and performing new tasks. It's like having a super-smart assistant who can help us with a variety of tasks. You can now begin to see how general AI is a big leap from narrow AI. It can suddenly help us explore so many new areas and become a trusted assistant or co-pilot.

Super AI

Now, let's talk about the big kahuna: Super AI! Imagine being able to ask a computer any question and having the answer provided right away. Or if you could give it a particularly challenging mathematical equation to solve, it would quickly solve it. All of that and a whole lot more would be possible with super AI! No problem, however complex, is beyond its capacity to solve. It is like having a genius on speed dial.

Scientists are still working on developing super AI, but it might take some time given how difficult it is. They want to make sure it is secure and has practical applications. They want to be extremely cautious and ensure that there won't be any issues that cause things to go wrong. We will get to the reasons why we need to be very careful while developing a capability like Super AI in a later chapter.

University research labs, companies, and the government are all spending millions of dollars every year on this research. And who knows? Perhaps we will soon have computers that are much smarter than anyone could have ever imagined. It is a fascinating concept to consider!

Now that we know what AI is, and what the different types of AI can do, it is important to understand that it took many years of research and the work of many brilliant minds to get here. In the next chapter, we will look at the brief history of AI.

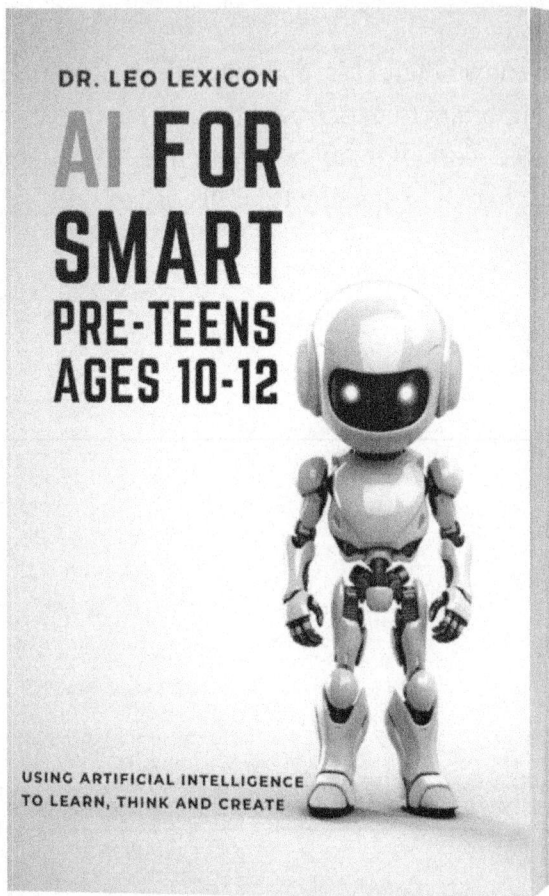

More titles for Smart Kids!

- Each book has over 40+ carefully curated HQ images
- Pefect companion for a road trip or vacation
- Try one today, you won't be disappointed
- Check out our other titles, we have all ages covered
- From the team at Lexicon Labs, bringing joy one page at a time!
- Follow Dr. Leo Lexicon on Twitter

@LeoLexicon

Printed in Great Britain
by Amazon